notes from the

Mother of the Bride
(m.o.b.)

planning tips and advice from a wedding-day veteran

notes from the

Mother of the Bride
(m.o.b.)

planning tips and advice from a wedding-day veteran

Sherri Goodall

SOURCEBOOKS CASABLANCA™
AN IMPRINT OF SOURCEBOOKS, INC.®
NAPERVILLE, ILLINOIS

This publication is designed to provide accurate and authoritative information in regard to the subject matter covered. It is sold with the understanding that the publisher is not engaged in rendering legal, accounting, or other professional service. If legal advice or other expert assistance is required, the services of a competent professional person should be sought.—*From a Declaration of Principles Jointly Adopted by a Committee of the American Bar Association and a Committee of Publishers and Associations*

All brand names and product names used in this book are trademarks, registered trademarks, or trade names of their respective holders. Sourcebooks, Inc., is not associated with any product or vendor in this book.

Published by Sourcebooks, Inc.
P.O. Box 4410, Naperville, Illinois 60567-4410
(630) 961-3900
FAX: (630) 961-2168
www.sourcebooks.com

Goodall, Sherri.
Notes from the mother of the bride (M.O.B.) : planning tips and advice from a wedding-day veteran / by Sherri Goodall.
p. cm.
ISBN 1-4022-0241-5 (alk. paper)
1. Weddings—Planning. 2. Wedding etiquette. I. Title.
HQ745.G66 2004
395.2'2—dc22

2004027649

Printed and bound in the United States of America
BG 10 9 8 7 6 5 4 3 2 1

To my BRIDE and joy, Denise

ACKNOWLEDGMENTS

I wish to express my profound appreciation to R.O.B., rabbi of the bride, Rabbi Marc Boone Fitzerman, for his valued opinions and for his unwavering faith in me. His words of encouragement carried me forward during my literary journey. Heartfelt thanks to Peggy Fielding, author, good friend, and my muse, who often stood behind me urging, "I believe in you—do it. Write!"

Thanks to Chef Harry Schwartz for his honesty, enthusiasm, suggestions, and for bringing Judy Martin into the picture. A special thanks to Judy, for becoming midwife and intrepid cheerleader to my idea.

Thanks to all those folks who helped me put on the finest wedding of my career.

Finally, I reserve my deepest appreciation for F.O.B. (father of the bride), my loving husband of thirty-some years—most of which seemed to occur the last few weeks prior to the wedding. He has kept me focused, encouraged, and laughing ever since our own wedding ceremony when he pledged his love by saying, "With this *wing*, I thee wed."

TABLE OF CONTENTS

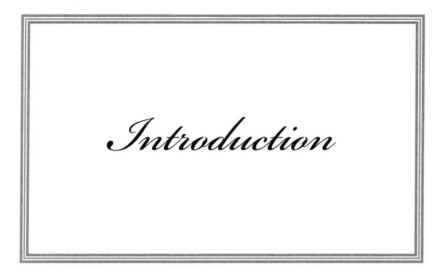

Introduction

During the course of my career as a party consultant, I had many opportunities to assist in planning weddings. However, when it was my turn to plan my daughter's wedding, I realized the person I coveted most as my professional confidante (another M.O.B.) was nowhere to be found.

Most books about wedding planning seemed dry and technical, and usually emanated from the wedding planner's or the bride's point of view. There were no humorous how-tos, especially from the mother-of–the-bride's mouth. So I decided to write my own.

You will find a list of really useful tips (R.U.T.s), time and budget planners, charts, and other helpful tools at the end of the book, many of which were gleaned from my thirteen years as a party store owner, planner, and, of course, as the M.O.B.

As with the birth of my bride, my thoughts for this book arrived when they wanted. Many of the ideas were written in the car, at traffic lights, in car washes, parking lots, on the back of deposit slips, on sales slips, napkins—whatever was handy at the time.

It's ninety degrees in Oklahoma. The special candy from New York is being shipped. "Dry ice in October…what, are you crazy?" from the mouth of the C.O.W. (Candy-Maker of the Wedding). So it goes.

I continue to write and laugh in hopes that this little tome will provide a few sorely needed chuckles and lots of helpful advice for other M.O.B.s.

A word about the acronyms: My rabbi and dear friend, Marc Boone Fitzerman, and I began communicating via voice mail, answering machines, secretaries, and email, signing off with "M.O.B." or "R.O.B." It then became a challenging game to find an acronym for everyone involved with the wedding.

A guide to the acronyms most often used in this book:
B. (Bride)
G. (Groom)
M.O.B. (Mother of Bride)
F.O.B. (Father of Bride)
R.O.B. (Rabbi of Bride)
M.E. (Main Event, wedding)
M.O.G. (Mother of Groom)
F.O.G. (Father of Groom)
E.P. (Event Planner, aka M.O.B.)

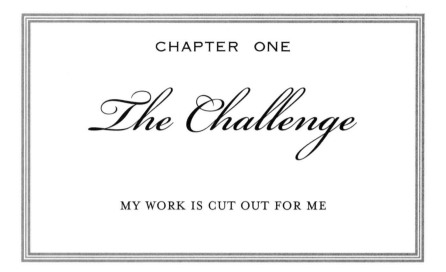

CHAPTER ONE

The Challenge

MY WORK IS CUT OUT FOR ME

The very first phase of my daughter's becoming a bride-to-be began with a generous dose of romance and sentiment. I knew I had to create and *plan* as I never had before to make this wedding *the* finish with a flourish.

The groom-to-be invited my husband, not yet the F.O.B., to "do lunch." The groom flew in for one day under wraps. I wasn't to know, nor was my daughter. My husband was a wreck, expecting some ominous news. The highly secret mission turned out to be an old-fashioned request for my daughter's hand in marriage. This genuinely thoughtful and respectful approach opened the door directly into F.O.B.'s romantic heart. After being helped up off the floor, the F.O.B. gave his permission enthusiastically. The new groom flew back to Ohio and to the unsuspecting object of his journey, my daughter.

That Saturday evening, said groom proposed on bent knee to my daughter in a penthouse suite awash in roses, candles, and starlight. This is the act I had to follow.

CHAPTER TWO

Sense and Sensibility

THE SENSIBLE WEDDING, AS OPPOSED TO THE
BLIND, EXCESSIVE, ORGIASTIC BLOWOUT GALA

If you read no further than this first sentence and learn your mantra—*Whose wedding is this anyway?*—you will have learned the most important lesson in this book.

Before you begin planning, determine the style of wedding the bridal couple wants.

Like the gown, the tux, and the shoes, the wedding has to "fit" the couple.

I know of couples who have taken their vows on a mountaintop or in a meadow, on Ferris wheels or in parachutes, in boats or in scuba gear in the sea. All it takes is imagination and a willing official.

Traditional weddings are still the most favored choice of bridal couples. There are varying degrees within the boundaries of tradition as with every style: champagne brunches in the morning with formal cutaway tuxedos and top hats; summer frocks and sport coats; formal or casual afternoon garden weddings followed by hors d'oeuvres or a seated dinner; and the ever popular *black-tie* evening gala where budget seems to have no boundaries.

If the wedding is to take place in a house of worship, certain rules of propriety will govern all elements such as ceremony, dress, music, and vows. Appropriate attire for a wedding in a church or synagogue is a far cry from what you'd wear to a wedding in a meadow where the bride dances down the hill in a see-through gauze frock with flowers in her hair and where the groom's best man is his dog.

Themes can be woven into the wedding. Consider carrying ethnic influences through with food, flowers, ceremony, and music. Some couples wish to create their wedding around a scene or locale evocative of a special moment in their lives. Specific themes can be echoed in everything from the ceremony to the reception centerpieces, cuisine, cake decor, and cocktail napkins. My daughter and son-in-law share the same last initial. I designed a heart with "G^2" in the corner. (It was a bit of a brain teaser unless you were a math major.) I used the logo on the napkins, the ice carving, and the chocolate heart truffles. Stamps can be inexpensively made to monogram many of the paper items, such as the guest book, napkins, and stationery. Today, with computers and printers, much of the wedding correspondence can be personalized right at your desk. Don't forget monogrammed personal items as a much-appreciated gift for the bridal party.

Once you've picked your style or theme, stick with it and sprinkle it throughout wherever possible, using good taste as your guide.

Ask your bride to shut her eyes and picture her fairy tale wedding. What does she see? Once she's shared her dream with you, check to see if you're both on the same planet and then proceed.

NOTES FROM THE M.O.B.:

Before we continue...should the bridal couple choose to elope, you're reading the wrong book.

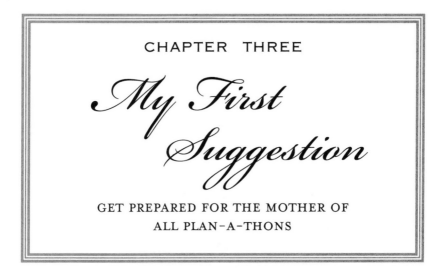

CHAPTER THREE

My First Suggestion

GET PREPARED FOR THE MOTHER OF
ALL PLAN-A-THONS

Brace yourself. This is the mother of all plan-a-thons, so get in shape. You might start by running the four-minute mile in several different directions at once. You will earn and give new meaning to the title *Wonder Woman*.

Launch yourself into the twenty-first century; buy a computer, an organizer, a fax, a cell phone, an answering machine, a memo minder, a few thousand sticky notes, and a prescription for Xanax.

Become a planning fool. Now the wedding, next the presidential inauguration!

If you want to become completely obsessed and a total recluse, go online and join the late-night wedding world—those folks who can't get enough stress during the day. Just hit "wedding" on your search engine and be prepared to be inundated with hundreds upon hundreds of wedding sites.

Speaking of online wedding sites, brides can register online for wedding gifts and create their own websites where they can communicate with their computer-blessed guests and bridal party. Since you'll always be taking your cue from the bride from this moment on, you might want to find out if she has already created a listserv or newsgroup for the bridal party. Maybe she'll let you join...

NOTES FROM THE M.O.B.:

For best results during the plan-a-thon (i.e., pre-M.E.),
take your feelings, put them in a box, and store them
on a shelf. They will only get in your way.

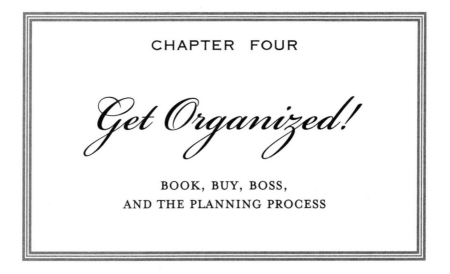

CHAPTER FOUR

Get Organized!

BOOK, BUY, BOSS,
AND THE PLANNING PROCESS

O rganization was the key to my sanity during the plan-a-thon. Hours tackled singly are so much easier to conquer than whole days. Whether you have one month or one year to plan the wedding, divide and prioritize your planning time into these three tiers: BOOK, BUY, BOSS.

First, BOOK:
- Book the church, synagogue, hotel, or mountain for the ceremony (and officiating personnel).
- Book the site for the reception, if different from ceremony.
- Book a wedding planner (if desired), caterer, baker (for the cake), florist, and musicians.
- Think about the guest list.

Next, BUY:
- Buy or order the gown, invitations, bridal party and bridesmaid dresses.
- Bridal couple registers for china, silver, and crystal; home and garden items; and other wished-for items.
- Think more about the guest list; write it in pencil.

Then, BOSS:
- Become the manager of all personnel you've hired and all products and services they've promised.
- Check and recheck order and shipping dates.
- Take a deep breath and write down the guest list in ink (you can always use white-out or hit the delete key).

Your Tools of the Trade:
1. Traveling Organizer
2. Home File

My Organizer

Purse-sized, large sections of Project Outline and Time Lines: *Things to do this month, this week, this day, this hour, TOO LATE...FORGET IT!*

I use my organizer constantly, checking off tasks accomplished, tearing out tasks impossible. I take notes everywhere I go and with everyone I meet concerning the M.E. I have the contacts section blown up so I can see phone numbers wherever I am. I constantly touch it, pat it—sort of like the B.'s blankie that she wouldn't let go of throughout kindergarten. We were certain it would end up tucked into the bridal bouquet (it didn't). I'm considering having my organizer preserved in bronze like my children's first shoes.

Of course, I have my guest list in my organizer at all times in case I get a sudden inspiration to delete someone.

I don't know how mankind managed before sticky notes. Neon sticky notes adorn my organizer, inside and out. The same sticky notes are yelling for attention from the dashboard of my car, the inside of my purse, on the rearview mirror, hanging on my keys. My car has become my office. The electronic voice reminder that F.O.B. bought me has been misplaced (lost) for weeks. I must confess to a rather strange reminder system of my own: it consists of strategically placed objects, or sticky notes, along the paths I most frequently travel. First priority is my makeup mirror, second might be the bathroom floor, next the back of the couch in my bedroom, then the hallway floor out to the living room, etc. The last bastion is the floor right in front of the door leading to the garage. If I don't see it, I trip over it. Moving anything can destroy a whole day's plan.

Your Organizer
Buy a three-ring 6 x 9–inch binder with inside pockets. I suggest you Velcro it to your body or have it surgically attached.

Your Organizer's Contents
- *Plastic business-card holder for your staff.* You are now the CEO of the M.E. (more about your role later).
- *Month-in-view calendar.* You can see at a glance what awaits you each month, each week, and each day. That's when you take your Xanax and take a deep breath. Kick yourself in the behind and GO GIRL! You can do this! (Do not, under any circumstances, go back to bed and pull the covers over your head!)

- *Project outline and things to do.* Specific projects like the flowers, cake, ceremony food, etc. will need to be broken down into detailed plans of action with estimated dates of completion. As you tackle and complete each project, date it and check it off. There is no greater feeling of accomplishment than checking off a project!
- *Notes.* Keep ideas and comments handy in notes section. It is a good place to add and delete guests and fill with sticky notes. You can further separate your note section into categories such as ceremony, reception, flowers, hospitality, etc.
- *Side pockets.* Keep a full supply of paper clips, pens, highlighters, Advil, and loads of sticky notes in the side pockets.

Your Home File

Along with my organizer, I have a legal-sized file at home. In it, I keep all materials applicable to the M.E. that do not need to travel with me, such as contracts, invoices, orders, and correspondence. Following is a suggested list of categories for your home file:

- Ceremony (processional order, music, clergy, recessional)
- Clothes
- Contracts
- Correspondence (letter to out-of-town guests—see Fig. 7; notes to bridal attendants re: rehearsals, fittings, etc.)
- Floral
- Food/bar/cake
- Guest lists
- Hospitality
- Ideas
- Invoices/receipts

- Music
- Photography/videography
- Reception (timetable of events, see Fig. 8)
- Registry
- Tables (sample of table chart, see Fig. 6)

NOTES FROM THE M.O.B.:

Velcro your traveling organizer to your body, or have it surgically attached.

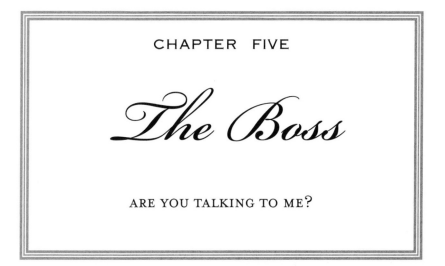

CHAPTER FIVE

The Boss

ARE YOU TALKING TO ME?

Now that you've assembled your team, booked, ordered, and bought all the wedding paraphernalia, it's time to be The Boss. You are The Boss of all those talented folks who will turn your dreams into a dazzling reality: unique invitations, heavenly ceremony, unforgettable flowers, ravishing reception with drop-dead decor, fabulous and flavorful food impeccably presented, a cake to swoon for, a Broadway band and clever favors…

All you have to do is manage the team. How do you do it?

BEING THE BOSS

The most important components of being a boss are:

   1. Delegate
   2. Delegate
   3. Delegate

4. Check and recheck orders and shipping progress
5. Praise

I cannot say enough for praise. One simply cannot overdo acknowledgment. I learned this in child-rearing classes as well as "puppy kindergarten." Our instructor told our class that if the neighbors didn't call the police, you weren't making enough of a fool out of yourself praising your puppy for making "potty" in the yard. Everyone working with and for you needs lots of praise. There were times when it was not easy to lavish praise. However, you would be surprised how quickly people rise to a compliment.

THE PLANNING PROCESS

The three most important components of the planning process are:
1. Time management
2. People management
3. Organizational skills

Once you break down this whale of a task into manageable parts, prioritize these parts, combine them, pare them down, and be mean and lean, you will find the overall journey much easier.

Here are several basic tenets of the planning process:
1. *Your mantra: Whose wedding is this anyway?* This is to be repeated often; if you don't say it to yourself, I guarantee someone else will...most likely the bride.
2. *"This too shall pass."* Say it often with your mantra.
3. *"Do not put things down, put them away."* This one has nothing to do with wedding planning, but it can't hurt. Besides, it's from my mother.

4. *Economy of movement*—perhaps the most important one of all. If you ever have found yourself in a room and don't know why, you are in good company. Studies have shown that when we overload our brains with too much information, we crash, just like our computers. We're not senile or Alzheimer's bound, just overwhelmed. It's the same principle behind taking a list to the grocery store…unless you enjoy wandering up and down every aisle hoping something will spark your memory. For fun, track yourself in your kitchen. How many times do you walk back and forth when one trip would suffice? With two arms, two hands, and ten fingers, it's amazing how many trips could be combined into one. This is where we prioritize, make lists, and stick to them. We pare it down and we become efficient!

5. *Your sense of humor.* Someday you really will look back, as I have, and laugh yourself silly.

6. *The big picture.* Decide which issues are worth going to battle over, and upon which hill you want to make your last stand. So many decisions become arenas for power contests between parents and bridal couples. Adults know the value of compromise. Don't use the $$$ thing as the final weapon.

Remember, in order to be an efficient planner, you have to be the master of organization. You have to manage people. You have to manage time.

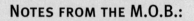

NOTES FROM THE M.O.B.:

Use your tools of the trade.

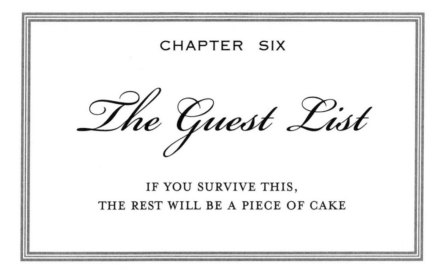

CHAPTER SIX

The Guest List

IF YOU SURVIVE THIS,
THE REST WILL BE A PIECE OF CAKE

I am often asked what the most difficult part of planning the wedding is. Hands down, it is THE GUEST LIST! This item will determine whether in-laws become out-laws.

Soon into the planning stage, we felt the kids were secretly putting ads in the classified personals: S.T.B.M.C.S.W.G.—A.T.W.W.D.: "Soon to be married couple seeking wedding guests—anything that walks will do." The bridal couple didn't feel it was much of a stretch to invite five hundred of their most intimate friends, as long as we were already pushing three hundred. What's another $two hundred people$? I drew the line at having to rent the convention center.

Actually, it turned out fine. Those people who are no longer speaking to us were probably looking for an excuse anyway. "Sure, *you* can walk away smiling. You don't have to live here. You're going to live in Ohio," I told my daughter.

F.O.B. suggested a lottery system: put all the names in a hat, draw out the first four hundred, and there's your list.

We met at least 150 of our wedding guests for the first time at the M.E.

F.O.B. and I looked at each other at the reception and said, "Who are all these people? I thought they were *your* family."

I have always believed one cannot have too many shoes, diamonds, or lists. So far I've only overdone lists. I have categorized the guest list on my computer from A (Alpha) to Z (Zip) and everything in between, including eye color, shoe size, fetishes, and diet. Now I can't even access them anymore. This, of course, does not include duplicates or the list F.O.B. keeps on his computer at his office. Today, nine days, five hours, and eleven minutes before the M.E., I have shredded seven bales of lists. What a great feeling, and I'm still secure. It's OK, everyone is still in at least four categories.

If you really want a small wedding, restrict your children to dating locals. Uniting two states spells B.M.W. (Big Massive Wedding) any way you look at it.

I never knew receiving regrets in the mail could lead to such elation!

The guest list, like every factor of your wedding, will be determined by your budget. I would suggest the following categories:

The "A" List
- Life-long friends
- Immediate family, ranging up to first cousins, depending on the size of your wedding, and the size of your family
- Obligatory business folks, i.e., your boss, important clients, etc.

The "B" List

- Casual friends, e.g., school, business, sports buddies, social pay-backs, etc.
- "Diaspora" family, e.g., third cousins you've met once
- Outer edge of business acquaintances, e.g., your doctor, dentist, postman, hairdresser (I consider hairdresser an "A" category), etc.
- Limit age of children to eight or ten years old

The "C" List

- Anyone you've ever been in class with, had a beer with, stood in line with, sat in a doctor's reception room with, or met on an airplane
- Anyone claiming to be related to you—their babies, children, grandchildren, and pets
- Anyone you've exchanged money with—cash, check, or charge

It isn't just the Hatfields and McCoys feuding. It can be the bride and her parents (usually the M.O.B.).

"I wouldn't know cousin Zelda if I fell in her lap! Why do we have to invite *her*? It's my wedding, it should be *my* friends!" This is where it can get ugly.

Step back, take a deep breath, be logical, be calm. Maybe you really don't have to invite cousin Zelda. Or better yet, explain why it is so important that you *do* invite her.

The definition of "family" will be different for everyone involved. Many battles have been fought over crazy Aunt Bertha who will arrive late, blow her nose during the ceremony, not send a gift, push her way through the food, but is a sister of the bride's mother, or first cousin Star with a ring in her nose and magenta hair.

Small weddings are a breeze. Everyone understands the limits of friends, family, and business obligations in the event of a small wedding.

Mega weddings are also a snap, usually given by royalty, the mega rich (same as royalty), and certain cultures that invite the whole town. The tricky part is remembering all those folks on the "C" list.

The most difficult and most popular are the midsized weddings, anywhere from seventy-five to two hundred people.

It is customary for whoever is giving the wedding (usually the bride's family), to determine the number of guests allowed to the groom's family. Often this number is a third or less than the bride's list. The reason for this is when the wedding is held in the bride's hometown, her family is obligated to more people. Grooms' families seldom understand this concept, so it is important to state the "rules" up front. In case of shared expenses by both families or exceedingly generous hosts, the guest list can be more evenly shared.

Once we determined the total number of guests, we gave half of the number to the bridal couple for their list. We shared the other half with the groom's parents. Many of the names were already on both lists, but we felt the bridal couple should have the "first" rights.

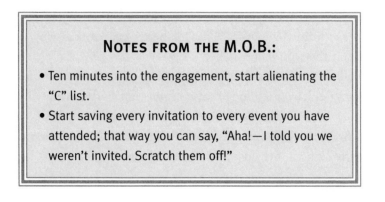

NOTES FROM THE M.O.B.:

- Ten minutes into the engagement, start alienating the "C" list.
- Start saving every invitation to every event you have attended; that way you can say, "Aha!—I told you we weren't invited. Scratch them off!"

CHAPTER SEVEN

The Band

A DIZZYING WEEKEND IN DALLAS
IN SEARCH OF *THE* BAND

One of your most important first calls, along with the butcher, the baker, the florist, and the candlestick maker, should be to the band. Our wedding date depended on the availability of these stars.

Soon after the engagement, the B. and G. told us they wanted *the* band (whatever that meant). The music would be a pivotal part of the reception—the music of today, no bubble machine. We headed to Dallas where we have a friend who is an Event Planner (E.P.)—the Ph.D. of party planners—involving events for ten to twenty thousand people, as in *conventions*.

Her mission was to drag us around Dallas for a weekend to hear all the best bands. Drag we did from club to club, mixing with the *crème de la crème* of Generation X. It's been way too long since F.O.B. and I did the disco scene…the noise, the tumult, the smoke, the weirdo dancing. Each time we arrived at a club, we just missed the "set" and would have to wait another half hour. F.O.B. said the last time we stayed out this late, the morning newspaper hit him in the back of the head as we came in our front door.

What we saw was an assortment of rangy creatures attired in clothes that could have come straight from my Cuisinart—rips, holes, missing sleeves. The headgear of choice was baseball caps with unprintable remarks worn backward. Various and assorted chains and rings adorned the bodies. "Don't worry," said our E.P., "they clean up real nice." Wedding gigs are where the real money is; no club owner in his or her right mind would pay these guys what we did.

We left…comatose, deaf, pleasantly high in a cloud of questionable smoke; it wasn't from Marlboros. The E.P. sent us home with actual videos from weddings. We didn't recognize most of the band members. These handsome young men in tuxedos couldn't be the same motley assortment we saw in Dallas. They not only "cleaned up real nice," but their music was fantastic. Our band threw in some oldies for me and F.O.B. The M.O.B. fancied herself a lyricist and rewrote the lyrics to *Oklahoma*. The band put it together, and at the reception we had the waiters pass out scrolls with the rewritten lyrics to all our guests. The crowd loved it; in fact, it was called for in several encores. The bridal couple knew nothing of my surprise. If they had, they would have nixed it as too "corny." It wasn't.

What type of music to have is solely determined by the style of reception before (yes, some folks have a reception prior to the ceremony, possibly with light hors d'oeuvres and violins) or after the wedding ceremony.

Morning weddings with brunch, lunch, or punch receptions call for background music at most, unless dancing is included in the celebration.

Houses of worship often have resident musicians: pianists, harpists, violinists, or vocalists. If one or any combination of musicians is used during the ceremony, they can often be hired to perform at the reception. If a band member has a specialty instrument that he/she plays, perhaps you can use that person to play during the cocktail hour or provide background music during food service.

If the reception is in the evening with dining, then dance music is appropriate. The range is vast—from disc jockeys to dynamite bands—and so is the expense.

Check with your church or synagogue. You'd be surprised how many closet musicians are hiding out there waiting to be discovered. What better venue for them than a wedding reception? High schools and colleges are another resource. Check with the music departments. Local bands abound. Again, a trip to the Yellow Pages or entertainment section of your newspaper will reveal their whereabouts.

Whomever you select, be sure to audition them. Be familiar with repertoires and style. Are they familiar with cultural music styles of the bridal couple? If possible, obtain references and check them.

Checklist for Your Band

1. Audition the band in person, preferably at a wedding. Obtain videos. References are reliable, depending on the source; hearing and seeing the group perform is best. Auditioning at clubs will give you some idea, but club settings are not weddings.
2. Read the contract. How many musicians and singers are included? How many hours will they play? How long will it take to set up? How many breaks will they take?
3. Are they familiar with the reception site?

4. What will they be expected to wear?

5. What songs will they play and in what order?

NOTES FROM THE M.O.B.:

Make sure musicians have an "itinerary" of the M.E.,
e.g., when bridal couple enters as "Mr. and Mrs.,"
toasts, first dance, intermissions, cake cutting, bouquet
tossing, etc. See Fig. 7 on p. 125.

CHAPTER EIGHT

The Wedding Gown

"SOMETHING BORROWED..."

I s there an article of clothing more impractical than a wedding gown? Spend a fortune, wear it once, spend another fortune to clean and preserve it, then relegate it to the far recesses of some closet or attic. Per square inch of fabric, nothing could prove less cost efficient.

Yet hundreds of thousands of women buy this article of clothing every year—after all, the Princess of the Day must feel like one! Whether you let extravagance or sensibility have its way, your daughter's reign as *The Bride* begins with that first silk-slippered step down the aisle in a walk like no other.

You know the ditty "something borrowed, something blue…?" Does your daughter have a future mother-in-law, sister, relative, good friend, or friend of a good friend that happens to have a wedding gown in her size? *Borrow it!*

How I wished my daughter wanted to wear my wedding dress. No such luck. Not only is this an economical solution, it's a sentimental one as well. I become teary eyed at the thought of a bride in her mother's gown…any bride, whether I know her or not.

Another cost-effective alternative to purchasing a gown is renting one. The Yellow Pages feature bridal boutiques that rent wedding gowns, bridesmaids' dresses, and M.O.B. dresses, as well as tuxedos.

Go online and check out www.discountbridalservice.com. Discount Bridal Service, or "DBS," is a mail-order company for brides. Savings amount to 20–40 percent off suggested retail for new, first-quality wedding gowns, accessories, and bridesmaid dresses. Brides need the manufacturer's name and the dress's style number, size, and color name or the page number of a favorite dress appearing in any of the bridal magazines. DBS verifies the style, gives you a price, and once ordered, the dress is shipped directly to the bride. Call DBS at (800) 874-8794. Try the dress on before ordering because there are no returns.

The newest kid on the block, along with the multitude of discount retailers, is the one-stop wedding store. Everything, except the bride and groom, is available from these purveyors: wedding-shower paraphernalia (games, decorations, invitations), wedding invitations, mementos, attendants' gifts, wedding decor, cake tops, and wedding attire. Most larger cities have such super stores.

I've noticed a burgeoning business in wedding-attire consignment shops. For a fraction of what the gown would cost new, you can buy gowns that have been worn before. If you really want to squeeze the last dollar out of the gown, reconsign it when you're finished.

Should you decide you must buy your gown new, allow yourself at least six months prior to your wedding day. Most gowns must be ordered and then altered.

This is one shopping expedition like no other. Study bridal magazines. Usually after you've tried on five or six dresses you'll know what fabric you're most comfortable with and what style looks best on you.

Speaking of wedding clothes, the bride's first fitting should occur when the dress arrives (assuming it's been ordered), usually three months prior to the wedding. The second and/or final fitting should take place no more than two weeks—preferably one week—before the wedding. Brides have a tendency to shed pounds until the last minute.

Have her wear bridal shoes around the house; test how they feel. She'll be in those puppies for about eight to ten hours.

Like ordinary clothing styles, wedding gowns debut each season. If you have enough time between the engagement and wedding, you can buy the gown on sale following the end of the season. Although traditional wedding gowns are less affected by dictates of season, a summer afternoon garden wedding in Atlanta would call for a different type of dress than a formal church wedding at Christmastime in Minnesota. Or buy a sample dress right off the rack at a bridal show. If you're lucky, it will fit the bride with minimum alterations. Be sure to dry-clean the dress before the wedding. You can save a good deal rather than purchasing the dress made to order.

Preserving your wedding gown requires a professional cleaner who knows how to handle the dress. Time is of the essence, especially if there are stains. Don't wait any longer than two weeks. Stains should be removed by hand and the dress turned inside out to protect delicate beadwork and embroidery. The most important facet of preservation is packing. The dress should be packed in an acid-free box with acid-free tissue paper. If there is a window in the box, it should be acetate, which is acid free (plastic is not acid free). Request that the headpiece be stored separately, since glue or metal parts can stain the dress. Your dress should be stored flat, not hung. Don't store your dress in an attic or basement, since these rooms may be damp or fluctuate in temperature.

Keep close tabs on attendants' clothes. Delays in ordering occur when groomsmen and bridesmaids do not provide measurements. It's part of the minutiae. Don't count on the *blissful couple* to do it. This is where your role as "the mother—*the nag*" comes into play. I appointed a "head" bridesmaid and "head" groomsman whom I knew were organized and responsible and asked them to oversee details of attendants ranging from clothes to rehearsals.

A word about the bridesmaids' dresses:

- Go with less frou-frou and more sophisticated and sensible (in fabric and design) so that the dress can be worn again.
- Allow bridesmaids to pick their own dress (with your bride's approval) all in the same color.
- Consider variations in hue in the same dress or even different dresses, as long as there is a sense of uniformity.
- Shoes and accessories such as gloves or shawls should be alike.
- A-line styles flatter most body shapes.

Checklist for Your Bridal Salon

1. Take photos of dresses with you to bridal salons.
2. Be clear about your budget. Only try on gowns within that budget. Include headpiece, veil, shoes, and jewelry in the budget.
3. Most bridal salons provide strapless bras. Inquire first so you can take along what you need.

4. Talk to the bridal salon employees about cleaning and preserving the gown after the wedding.

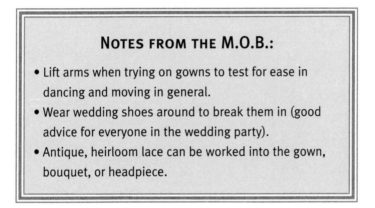

NOTES FROM THE M.O.B.:

- Lift arms when trying on gowns to test for ease in dancing and moving in general.
- Wear wedding shoes around to break them in (good advice for everyone in the wedding party).
- Antique, heirloom lace can be worked into the gown, bouquet, or headpiece.

CHAPTER NINE

The Kleinfeld Experience

THE MARATHON OF ALL SEARCHES:
THE WEDDING GOWN

I realized we were in deep trouble as thirty of us brides and mothers of the brides boarded the van to Brooklyn—all having the same 2:00 P.M. appointment at Kleinfeld Bridal Salon.

As we were told to have a seat in a lobby the size of my bedroom, I started my de-e-ep breathing (something I've mastered). I got that "look" from my daughter, the one that says "Mother, don't you dare…"

At 2:47 P.M., I marched up to the receptionist and announced that we had traveled thousands of miles from Oklahoma for this appointment, and if they couldn't keep it, I wanted a car to take me back to the city for an appointment with another well-known bridal salon. With one raised eyebrow the receptionist replied, "We have clients here from Japan and Saudi Arabia—and *you're* complaining?"

At 2:51 P.M., the same receptionist, hoping to soothe the restless M.O.B.s, ceremoniously served us butter cookies in the lobby. At 2:59

P.M. our names were called and we were ushered into our private room with our personal bridal consultant who was wonderful. At this point we were ready for anything. We found it slightly peculiar though, to see our bridal consultant sprouting large metal clothespins from her body. These clothespins are the ingenious solution to fitting a sample size eight to every possible bridal body. We witnessed the most amazing retrieval of gowns from an airplane-hangar sized room of inventory by wizards garbed in jeans and black Kleinfeld T-shirts.

One of these gowns became the gown of my bride's dreams.

For her shopping attire, my bride chose ankle length stonewashed blue jeans, no holes, designed by Levi's. Her bodice was a matching denim shirt with a button-down collar by J. Crew. On her feet she wore black Dr. Martens (aka combat boots). Completing her ensemble was a headpiece made of a covered rubber band that gathered her hair into a ponytail. She probably would have had difficulty getting into a PG-13 movie. The M.O.B. struggled to keep her mouth shut, especially about the Dr. Martens (imagine *those* underneath a wedding gown). I was shocked to see almost every other bride-to-be in the identical outfit, down to the shoes.

Once dressed in the gowns, we paraded out into a small arena covered in mirrors. Each bride perched on a platform (similar to the ones circus elephants perform upon), where she was able to see herself from every angle. Of course, every mother present seemed besotted by her own daughter's beauty (including me), knowing *without a doubt!* that hers (mine) was *the* bride of perfection. The combined *kvelling* (Yiddish for *gloating*) was enough to send all of Brooklyn to heaven. As if on cue, the moment the veil was put on my bride, my tears began. The bridal consultant looked at her watch and said, "Yes…that's just about the time they cry."

What an enterprise! Once the gown is selected, just a short hop away are the M.O.B. dresses. Of course, bridal jewelry, bridal shoes, and bridal underwear were part of the bait. Down the street, if one could still stand up, bridesmaids' dresses awaited. The lure of all this necessary paraphernalia within three square blocks was simply irresistible. All that was lacking was a catering department.

Kleinfeld closes at 6:00 P.M. At 7:15 P.M., they swept us off the floor and out the door, having sold us one bridal gown, one headpiece with a veil, two pairs of shoes, eight bridesmaids' dresses, one pair of earrings, and a partridge in a pear tree. I left with visions of my bride floating in yards of scrumptious lace, satin, and silk, awash in a sea of pearls—with Dr. Martens on her feet.

NOTES FROM THE M.O.B.:

If taking the Kleinfeld route, make your appointment during the week. Saturdays are very busy.

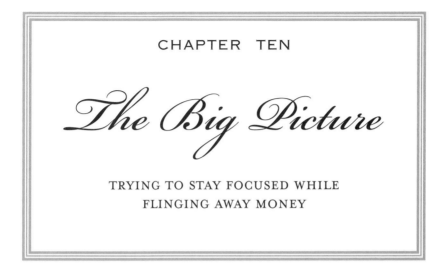

CHAPTER TEN

The Big Picture

TRYING TO STAY FOCUSED WHILE
FLINGING AWAY MONEY

Close your eyes and imagine yourself in your twilight years (immediately following wedding) hooked up to your VCR like an intravenous lifeline, reliving each memory on your $wedding video$. Speaking of $$...today's wedding and reception can cost somewhere between one hundred dollars to two hundred dollars per person, depending on how you plan to water, feed, and entertain your guests. One hundred fifty well-cared-for guests could set the hosts back at least thirty thousand dollars...and that's just the reception.

My loving sister-in-law, who recently experienced her third M.E. (this wedding took place high in the hills overlooking the Pacific Ocean, nestled on the side of a golf course; every few minutes an errant golf ball or a golfer's unprintable exclamation would sail past the ceremony), told me repeatedly during the plan-a-thon, "Don't lose sight of the *big picture.* In the whole scheme of things, when it's all said and done, what's two more $people$? Who will even notice the moiré $tablecloths$ that are made new for each occasion?" (Reused—never!)

"Excuse me, that $price$ does *not* include shipping?" says shocked M.O.B.

Who will remember the $gilded rose petals$; the $monogrammed$ candy, napkins, guest towels; and the matching $ice carving–cum–vodka bar$? Besides me and F.O.B., the only people who will remember will be the suppliers of all these things into whose pockets we shoveled money.

Yes, I was to think of the big picture always. When my daughter, in her calm, evenly modulated voice would shriek, "Oh my God, Mother, you're doing *what?*" Think of the big picture. Or the F.O.B., with his daily litany, "Nothing, I said, nothing can cost this much. The President's inauguration didn't cost this much. Princess Di's wedding didn't cost this much. Anybody out there hear me?" Think of the big picture.

NOTES FROM THE M.O.B.:

Keep the budget handy. Refer to it often. It is so easy to get carried away with $details$. Weigh some of your wishes against reality and decide if the "extras" are really necessary.

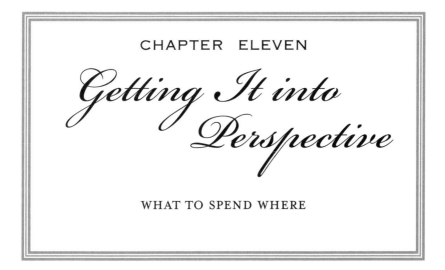

I know of a couple with four daughters. Each was presented with the same budget for her wedding. They were told to pick the one component they felt most significant to their dream wedding.

One chose the flowers and had the wedding in the backyard, which was tented and transformed into a floral fairyland. Another chose the wedding attire. She was bedecked in a magnificent Victorian-style wedding gown. Her attendants were children—a tradition common in Europe—dressed in velvet pantaloons, gold slippers, and ribbons. A horse-drawn carriage transported the bride. The third married an Italian and chose food. She had an Italian feast where several chefs at different stations cooked every type of Italian cuisine from antipasto to zabaglione. The fourth decided a drop-dead band was the key and spent the majority of her budget creating a laser-lit disco featuring a well-known band.

It is important to step back occasionally and see your forest for the trees. You are giving the party of your life. Cater to your guests, not yourself. What memories do you want them to take home?

Will your guests remember monogrammed napkins and moiré table-cloths before they remember what they ate? Will they reminisce about fabulous flowers before they recall the sentimental ceremony? If the music was great, they'll remember; if it wasn't, they'll also remember. And the ice carving…will it melt before it's noticed?

Think of weddings you have attended. What do you remember?

I remember the bride always. Each one is gorgeous in her own unique beauty. The dress is important, but not above the bride. The dress is the adjective; the bride is the noun. If the ceremony was particularly touching and romantic, I remember it. As for the food, I only remember it if it was terrible. I remember presentation before I remember taste.

Details, details, details…you are creating a tableau. Each piece completes the whole. It truly is all "in the details." When "it" works, all the pieces fit smoothly together. There are no ragged edges or pieces that stick out loudly.

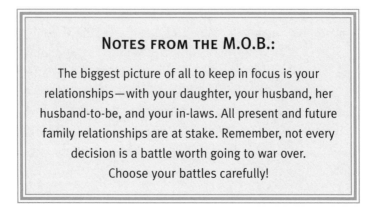

NOTES FROM THE M.O.B.:

The biggest picture of all to keep in focus is your relationships—with your daughter, your husband, her husband-to-be, and your in-laws. All present and future family relationships are at stake. Remember, not every decision is a battle worth going to war over. Choose your battles carefully!

CHAPTER TWELVE

Flowers, Food, Champagne...

...AND OTHER NECESSARY EVILS

THE FLOWERS

White roses carried against candlelight silk—visual senses synonymous with brides for centuries. Who can forget Princess Di's bridal bouquet? Her thirty-pound cascade of white roses, white orange blossoms, and green laurel proclaimed innocence, hope, and purity.

Today's bride is not afraid to gather an armful of vivid wildflowers and transform them into her bridal bouquet. What must be remembered is this: as with the gown, the bouquet is an adjective; the bride is the noun.

We women remember the flowers. Talented florists can create the illusion of bountiful bouquets with fewer precious flowers and more filler such as ivy or baby's breath. Trust the "less is more" principle. Loose wildflowers carried in the crook of the arm as opposed to structured bouquets are ever popular and cost less money. Simple elements gathered together make spectacular statements. Imagine one noble, exquisitely wrapped calla lily held simply at the waist or dried flowers carried in a basket or on the arm. Be aware of the time of year; try to choose flowers in season. Roses and orchids in December are ravishing but oh so costly. Come to think of it, Valentine's Day should be in May! Try to use locally grown flowers. Visit your local floral wholesaler if you want to eliminate the cost of a florist.

Don't be afraid to recycle your flowers and use them for more than one event. Freshen up the rehearsal dinner flowers and use them for the wedding reception. Many brides arrange the bridesmaids' bouquets on the reception, gift, and cake tables.

Types of Bouquets

The *cascade* is the largest of all the bouquets, composed of flowers loosely flowing downward to a point resembling a cascading waterfall. Traditionally, white roses, stephanotis, and white lilies are used in the cascade. Greenery is used to pull the look together.

The *biedermeier* or *round-cluster bouquet* (sometimes called a *nosegay*), is the most traditional of bouquets. Stems are removed and replaced with taped wire, allowing construction of a precise ring of flowers, usually roses. Color is often used here in varying, compatible hues. Very little or no greenery is used. Loops of ribbon under the bouquet provide a colorful backdrop as well as a carrying handle for the bride.

The *hand-tied* or *loose-tied bouquet* is less formal than the other types and most favored in summer and springtime when colorful varieties abound. The bouquet is "casually" gathered and often secured with flowing ribbons. For a more formal look, elegant, long-stemmed blooms may be used—calla lilies, roses, hydrangeas—with French braided ribbons wrapping their stems. The bouquet usually nestles in the crook of the arm, similar to the flowers Miss America carries.

Checklist for Your Florist

1. What flowers are in season the month of your wedding?
2. Bring a picture of the bride's gown and a fabric swatch to the florist. Bring pictures of bridal bouquets. Talk about style and color. Talk about your daughter's "vision" of herself as a bride, of her wedding.
3. Have the florist view ceremony and reception sites well in advance of the wedding. Discuss lighting.
4. Order a "tossing" bouquet.
5. Have the florist bring extra boutonnieres and loose flowers for emergencies.
6. Present your floral budget and stick to it!

NOTES FROM THE M.O.B.:

- Use the bridal bouquet and bridesmaids' bouquets to dress the cake table, gift table, reception cards table, etc.
- Use the mini version (rose bud, baby calla lily) of bridal flowers for the groom's boutonniere. His corsage harks from the eighteenth century tradition of the groom plucking one stem from his bride's bouquet and placing it in his buttonhole (*boutonniere* in French).
- If choosing fragrant flowers, consider allergies.

Preserving the Bridal Bouquet

Refrigerate the bouquet until it goes to a florist to be professionally preserved. Professionals usually air dry or freeze dry bouquets.

To preserve the bouquet at home: Hang bouquet the upside down in a cool, dry, dark place to minimize color loss. After ten days to two weeks, the entire bouquet can be sprayed (ribbons, lace, and all) with a floral preservative. They may also be dipped in Craft-Flex to give them a porcelain veneer. If used for potpourri, remove the individual dried petals, spray them with floral preservative, and put them in a glass container. Scented oils and spices may be added. The oils may damage containers other than glass or crystal.

Flowers preserved in silica gel crystals hold their color better than those that are air-dried. Gel crystals and preservative sprays can be found at craft stores.

To press the bouquet, take the larger flowers apart, saving the petals. Press the smaller flowers and the individual petals between clean paper (white tissue will work) using heavy books as weights. It takes at least three to four weeks for the flowers to dry. Carefully peel flowers from the paper when dried and glue them to parchment paper in an arrangement evocative of the bridal bouquet. Proper glues can be found at craft stores. Many brides add the groom's boutonniere, a bridesmaid's flower, and the wedding invitation and put the entire arrangement behind glass for display.

THE REFRESHMENTS

Make refreshments one of your top priorities. It makes more sense to provide less variety and the best of what you can rather than lots of inferior food. If you are serving a complete dinner, think about quality, not quantity; do you need appetizers, soup, and salad? If you have a scrumptious cake, do you need other desserts? Again, time of day dictates menu, thus expense.

I've attended morning weddings followed by light brunch, evening weddings followed by formal, sit-down dinners, and everything in between. Buffets are often less expensive than served plates even though food amounts are equal; the presentation costs more when individually prepared and served.

If hors d'oeuvres are served, choose items easily handled (not extreme temperatures or messy consistencies). If a sauce is within six feet of me, I guarantee it will find a home on my dress...and chocolate need only be in the same building to wind up sharing my clothes. Using waitpersons to pass hors d'oeuvres can be more economical than free-for-all buffets, since you can control how much food is put on each tray.

It is important to decide whether alcohol will be served and, if so, to what extent? Be prepared. If full bars are offered, the "spirits" bill could easily equal the food bill. Hosts frequently offer one glass of champagne for the bridal toast. Another alternative is to serve a champagne punch. If you choose to have an open bar, it's a good idea to designate the time it will be open. When the meal is served, wine is usually served and the bar is closed. If wine is poured, instruct the waitpersons to ask if refills are desired; otherwise rivers of wine are wasted, along with many of the guests. It's a good and safe idea to close the alcohol service an hour before the end of the reception.

Choosing a caterer is as personal as choosing your doctor or decorator. Personalities and tastes have to click. Sampling his or her cuisine is the best measure of a caterer's talent. The next-best indicator is several recommendations by satisfied clients.

Checklist for Your Caterer

1. If you're not using a wedding planner, then your caterer will be your reception "foreman." He or she will have to work with the florist, band, food service, and servers.

2. Price per guest usually *does not include gratuity and tax.* Factor these in when determining budget. Does price include tablecloths, napkins, etc.?

3. Is the caterer familiar with the reception site and the kitchen facilities?

4. Ask for a sample menu and tasting. Ask that tables be set with linens, folded napkins, and china as planned for the wedding (good time for florist to set sample table arrangement).

5. How many waitpersons will there be? What will they wear?

6. If you are serving alcohol, how many bartenders will there be and what will they cost? Select call brands for liquor.

THE CAKE

This is not your mother's wedding cake. Gone are the plastic bride-and-groom cake toppers—thank goodness.

Cakes today are works of art worthy of display in a museum. However dazzling, the defining measure of the cake's success will be its taste. The most sought-after bakers agree that the ingredients they use are what separates them from commercial bakers.

Gumpaste, a type of frosting that can be handmade into lace, baubles and beads, ribbon swags and curls (indistinguishable from their real counterparts), is the signature of the true cake artiste. It is this intricate and exquisite attention to detail that transforms the white wedding cake into a spectacular "*ooh* and *ah*" creation.

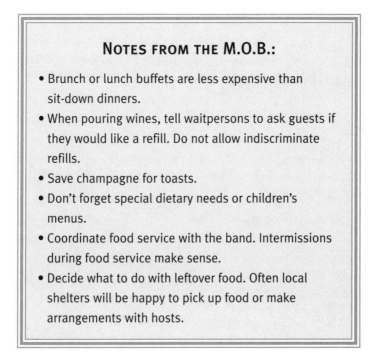

NOTES FROM THE M.O.B.:

- Brunch or lunch buffets are less expensive than sit-down dinners.
- When pouring wines, tell waitpersons to ask guests if they would like a refill. Do not allow indiscriminate refills.
- Save champagne for toasts.
- Don't forget special dietary needs or children's menus.
- Coordinate food service with the band. Intermissions during food service make sense.
- Decide what to do with leftover food. Often local shelters will be happy to pick up food or make arrangements with hosts.

Cakes in the shape of wrapped presents are popular. The layers, or "boxes," are stacked one on top of the other. The icing "wrapping" is what makes these cakes so dramatic. Lattice work, pearls, lace, ribbons, and bows created from icing adorn the gift-wrapped boxes. Scatter real flowers on and around the cake. Certain flowers are edible as well as decorative, such as pansies and certain varieties of rose petals.

Many brides opt for more unusual arrangements, such as stacked layers at different levels or layers fanned out in swirls separated by elaborate crystal columns, mounds of roses, or mini fountains. Brides will sometimes try to echo a design element of their dress in the design of the cake or carry out a theme with initials or flowers.

Many of the smaller, more-elaborate cakes featured in magazines not only would be frighteningly expensive but next to impossible to duplicate on a large scale. One way to "have your cake and eat it too" is to display a "show" cake with a real bottom layer for the ceremonial cut. After the cutting ceremony, the "show" cake is whisked away and guests are served from sheet cakes made with the same ingredients (presliced in the kitchen).

Whimsy or informality is usually saved for the groom's cake, chocolate being the most popular flavor. Fanciful designs with few limits are the rule with the groom's cake (sports insignia, cigars, body parts (ahem), geography, fraternity letters, etc.). Many couples choose to send home a piece of the groom's cake as a favor. Tradition has it that a single woman slipping the piece of groom's cake under her pillow (keep it in the box!) will dream of her future husband.

Cake tasting is just as important as your food tasting. You'll want a cake as delicious as it looks.

Frostings

Fondant icing is made from pure sugar and has the consistency of Play-Doh when rolled out. The technique comes from Australia. It has a hard, matte finish resembling porcelain; it can be colored and flavored. In the hands of an artist, rolled fondant can be fashioned into anything the heart desires: butterflies, lace, beads, flowers, bows, baskets, etc. It takes enormous talent to work fondant into breathtaking décor; thus it is can be quite costly. Gumpaste is hardened fondant, and is always used to create exquisite designs to grace fondant-iced cakes.

The basics of *buttercream* are butter, egg whites, and sugar. The texture is creamy yet firm. When in the hands of an expert, buttercream can be smooth as glass or sculpted into silklike flowers, woven baskets, swags, lacy bows, or made to look like fabulously wrapped presents. Every inch of décor, whether baubles or beads, must be hand-piped onto the cake. Because of the delicate nature of buttercream, bakers prefer to use real flowers to top the cake rather than sculpted ones. Buttercream is much tastier and less time intensive than fondant, thus more requested by brides.

Ganache is usually made from chocolate (white or regular) and beaten with heavy whipping cream. It is not usually used for bridal cakes but rather for the groom's cake. It gives a beautiful shiny and smooth look to the cake.

Remember, outdoor receptions, especially in summer, can cause fondants to melt, buttercreams and ganaches to sweat, and custard and cream fillings to spoil.

Preserving the Cake Top

If possible, refrigerate the cake top overnight. Remove flowers and top pieces. Gumpaste flowers can be stored in a cabinet. Wrap the cake in a double layer of plastic, then place it in a plastic bag, box it, and tape it shut. Defrost it by placing it in the refrigerator overnight so that it doesn't sweat and lose moisture. It should taste as good as it did on the wedding day.

Checklist for Your Baker

1. Is cost figured on whole cake or by the piece? Does cost include transporting and set-up of the cake?

2. Discuss length of time the cake will be sitting out. Will it be inside, outside, in front of windows, etc.? Do your homework—familiarize yourself with different fillings and different types of icing.

3. Bring pictures of cakes, your gown, or anything personal you'd like to incorporate in the cake décor. Ask to see pictures of the baker's work.

4. If fresh flowers are to be used, coordinate with the florist and the baker.

5. Ask about ingredients. Expect a tasting.

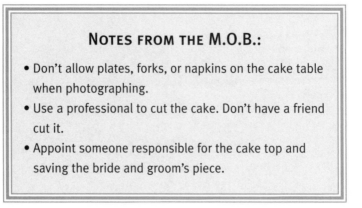

NOTES FROM THE M.O.B.:

- Don't allow plates, forks, or napkins on the cake table when photographing.
- Use a professional to cut the cake. Don't have a friend cut it.
- Appoint someone responsible for the cake top and saving the bride and groom's piece.

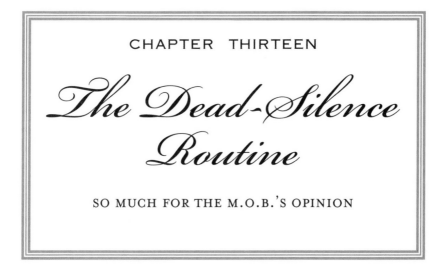

A fter so many episodes of this typical exchange:

M.O.B. to B.: "I've got this fantastic idea about the...

    1. wedding program."

    2. candy."

    3. hospitality room."

    4. band."

    5. ceremony."

    6. flowers."

    7. world hunger."

    8. none of the above."

    B. to M.O.B.: *dead silence*

    ...you'd think that one would probably catch on and devise a different approach. I never did. Those silences became little roadblocks, requiring split-second alternate routes. Either rephrase the whole idea, drop the subject, make it seem like it is her idea, or, as a last resort, kill the thought.

Your job description is to be the calm center of this frenetic whirlwind of activity.

During a trip to Spain two years before the M.E., the F.O.B. and I bought a beautiful silver antique ceremonial wedding ring. I pictured this ring being used during my daughter's wedding ceremony—how meaningful it would be, how unusual. I presented the idea a dozen different ways, eliciting the same response every time—dead silence. The ring is still in my drawer.

Consider the fact that brides are marrying older today, have lived away from their hometowns for several years, have careers, have formed new business and social groups, and you may wonder why they need an M.O.B. at all. Often the bride decides to marry in her city of residence rather than her hometown. This creates a situation for the M.O.B. that makes a wedding planner more important than ever unless she's prepared to plan a wedding long distance—a very difficult proposition. If the bride has the time, of course, she can make the arrangements. If she's among the career women of the twenty-first century, she won't have time. Wedding consultants have access to all the wedding vendors, and their job is to ride herd on every one of them. The M.O.B.'s role, in this instance, is to be the Chief Operating Officer of the M.E. Her Chairman of the Board will be the wedding planner.

The M.O.B. needs to recognize her bride's status as an adult, her level of maturity and sophistication. On the other hand, daughters must recognize that their mothers have been around the block a few times. In the process, we mothers have acquired experience and wisdom that our daughters just don't have yet. Taste is a different matter! We mothers know daughters need us, no matter the age. Mutual respect for each other's role is essential for a smooth working relationship.

My mother did it all. I was in college and was incapable of thinking much beyond my studies. F.O.B. was busy being important in the world of business; furthermore, he is color blind so couldn't be bothered with banal decisions regarding wedding details. Our son-in-law is a man of impeccable taste…after all, he chose my daughter as his bride! However, he would have wanted to be involved in every detail of the wedding had we allowed it. He was the one I cut my teeth on regarding the "don't ask for an opinion unless you are really going to listen" rule. We operated on a "need to know" basis. I was the imperial umpire deciding who needed to know what.

There comes a time when instinct takes over and you learn to make "executive decisions," aka keeping your mouth shut and doing it anyway. As the mother, you'll know when.

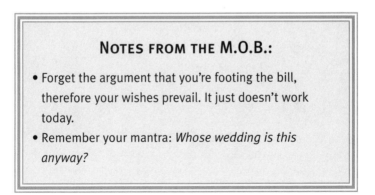

NOTES FROM THE M.O.B.:

- Forget the argument that you're footing the bill, therefore your wishes prevail. It just doesn't work today.
- Remember your mantra: *Whose wedding is this anyway?*

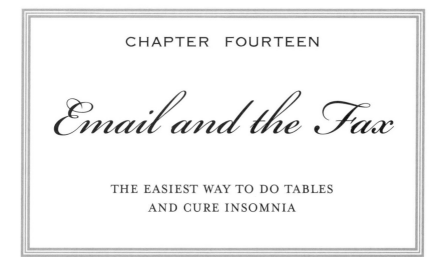

CHAPTER FOURTEEN

Email and the Fax

THE EASIEST WAY TO DO TABLES
AND CURE INSOMNIA

I f you're an insomniac, get on your computer and get a fax machine.

My family and good friends know that I am a world-class insomniac. Lack of sleep is nothing novel for me. One to four hours a night is about the best I can do. This leaves some major "down time." My big worry is knowing that one needs less sleep as he or she ages. I fear that soon I'll be in the negative column. I suppose I can always acquire a newspaper route or open a doughnut shop. Let's hope I can stay awake by the time I have to walk down the aisle and not nod off during the ceremony.

The beauty of the fax and email is that I have something to do in the middle of the night. Never mind that the rest of the world slumbers. I can fax and email my brains out; no one need be there to receive. I couldn't wait for M.O.G. to get her fax machine so we could do tables at 3:00 A.M.

Unfortunately, it took almost three weeks for M.O.G. to get her fax machine up and running. Either she could transmit but not receive or receive but not transmit. This made doing tables a bit difficult; for that matter doing anything was difficult. At the eleventh hour, a miracle occurred: her fax received and transmitted. I felt like Alexander Graham Bell making contact for the first time. Our tables were done within hours.

As long as we're talking twenty-first century technology, do you have a computer? If the answer is "yes", are you online? If you answer "yes" to the last question, then you'll have the capability of planning the entire wedding without leaving your ergonomically correct chair!

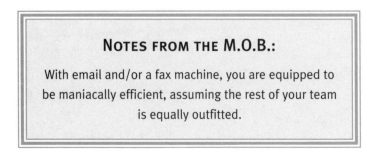

NOTES FROM THE M.O.B.:

With email and/or a fax machine, you are equipped to be maniacally efficient, assuming the rest of your team is equally outfitted.

CHAPTER FIFTEEN

Ten Commandments for the M.O.G.

(Mother of the Groom)

THOU SHALT WEAR BEIGE AND KEEP THY MOUTH SHUT

THE TEN COMMANDMENTS

1. Thou shalt wear beige and keep thy mouth shut. Perhaps a bit harsh, but remember the corollary to the first commandment: he and/or she that giveth the bride away along with bucketfuls of money shall giveth all other commands.
2. Thy dress shall be lovely but not drop-dead gorgeous.
3. Thy prenuptial dinner shall feature good food, fun, and festivity, but shall not be to-die-for fabulous. (Same for thy flowers, invitations, etc.)
4. There shall be space for two prima donnas at the very most. Thou art not one of them.
5. Wedding toasts and roasts shall be given by thy hosts.
6. Thou shalt not utter the phrase, "If it were me, I would have done it this or that way…" to anyone on the bride's side, especially the M.O.B.

7. Thou shalt not expect a postwedding, next-morning phone call from thy baby boy.

8. Thou shalt ferry thy son to the altar in one reasonably sober piece, especially if there has been a bachelor party the night before.

9. Thou shalt hope for granddaughters. Thou may be a star at that wedding.

10. If thou help giveth the wedding, disregard all of the above except numbers five and eight.

MY STINT AS THE M.O.G.

I had the honor and pleasure of being the M.O.G. at my son's wedding a couple of years after my daughter's wedding. I got an A in wearing beige. I flunked keeping my mouth shut. (Remember the mantra: *Whose wedding is this anyway?*)

The Saga of the Tux Shirt

Sunday, 9:20 A.M.—a Ritz-Carlton hotel, somewhere in the Midwest.

Forty minutes before photos, two hours before his noon wedding, my son walks into our hotel room. "Mom, I don't know how to tell you this…"

I'm afraid to even look at him, but when I do there he is in all his handsome tuxedoed glory—sleek, model body in a designer tux jacket; silver embroidered vest; matching bow tie; striped pants; shiny, patent-leather tux shoes—and no shirt.

"There's no tux shirt," my son, the groom, informs me as if I were blind. "I thought you were supposed to get it," he continues.

"What do you mean? *You* were supposed to get it," I answer.

This repartee goes on for about fifty seconds.

"Stop!" I command. "This conversation is getting us nowhere fast."

F.O.G. is standing in the middle of the room, shaking his head in disbelief.

I call the concierge to ask what time the dozens of fashionable men's stores right across the street open.

"Noon."

"Oh, no." I'm thinking, *there were two weddings last night at the hotel. I saw several groomsmen leave their tuxes with the concierge…*

"Do you still have the tuxes from the weddings last night?" I ask.

"Yes, Madame."

"Surely there is a shirt in the group that will fit my son. I don't care if it's dirty, wrinkled—just so it's white!"

Just about the time I'm convulsing, the florist walks in the room. He hears me explain our predicament to the concierge—groom, noon wedding, Sunday, no tux shirt.

"My roommate is about your son's size, 17/34?" my florist says as he joins the hysteria. "I live five minutes away." He flies off.

"Madame," the concierge replies calmly. "The staff at the Ritz-Carlton wears tuxedoes. It is our uniform. What size does your son wear? Does he prefer a wing collar or pointed? I'll send some up."

Within fifteen minutes, we have four clean, pressed shirts to choose from.

I can't believe our luck.

I throw my arms around the florist and the concierge.

"Tell me the truth. Is this the first time this has ever happened?" I ask.

"No, Madame. We've had to provide complete tuxes before, even shoes. Yours was easy."

When we arrived for photos completely attired, the rabbi stops me. "Do you by any chance have your son's marriage license?"

"Rabbi, I just pulled four tux shirts out of thin air; I don't think I can perform another miracle. It's your turn."

Notes from the M.O.B.:

The M.O.G. plays a supporting role to the bride and her mother. It can be a dicey role at that. Knowing your obligations beforehand is very helpful.

CHAPTER SIXTEEN

Ten Commandments for the F.O.B.
(Father of the Bride)

MAKING A FASHION STATEMENT HAS ITS PRICE

THE TEN COMMANDMENTS

1. Thou shalt buy or rent a fashionable tuxedo; wearing the one from thy cruise ten years ago is not acceptable.
2. Thou shalt refer to the groom as thy future "son-in-law," not "what's-his-name."
3. Thou shalt banish the words "in my day" from thy vocabulary.
4. Thou shalt not expect an invitation to the bachelor party; thou shalt not grumble and whine about it.
5. Thou shalt have the honor of giving the first toast to the bridal couple…thou shalt not accompany them to the honeymoon suite.
6. Thou shalt be allowed a private moment with the bride before thy walk down the aisle.
7. Thou shalt understand fathers never truly "give their little girl (aka the bride) away."

8. Thou shalt count to one hundred slowly before cutting in on the first dance of the bridal couple.

9. Thou shalt recognize the hallowed position of the M.O.B. up to and during the wedding and defer all critical decisions to Her Highness.

10. Thou shalt take thy Prozac faithfully, especially when the bills arrive.

FOIBLES OF THE F.O.B.

For the F.O.B., the entire month of September was one bad shopping day.

It began when, en masse, the B. and G. and their parents went to New York. The B. had the rest of the Kleinfeld experience left—the fitting. The M.O.G. had a fitting on her dress, and the guys decided to visit a famous Italian designer for their tuxedos. I went along as ringmaster.

We gathered at dinner the first evening after having gone our respective ways. The F.O.B. smugly announces that Guido, the manager of the famous Italian salon, has convinced him that "he (F.O.B.)...and *only he*, must wear the newest European state-of-the-art tuxedo." Unlike the G. and F.O.G., who opted for shawl collars and single-breasted tuxedos, the F.O.B. is going to make a fashion statement in a wide-lapel, double-breasted, long-line Italian creation. I am very, *very* uneasy and suggest a visit to Guido the next morning. "No, no, Guido says I look *magnifico*," the F.O.B. insists.

So we head back to Oklahoma. We've done the ordering part; now we do the waiting part.

The moment of truth arrives along with the FedExed tuxedo. The F.O.B. puts it on. In a carefully controlled voice, I screech, "You're going to walk down the aisle in *that?* You look like Spike Jones! Does 'zoot suit' mean anything to you?" I've made my point because we are soon on the phone with Guido whose head I'm demanding on a pasta platter. We make each other offers we cannot refuse, and within forty-eight hours a shawl collared, single-breasted tuxedo arrives on our doorstep.

This near disaster was shortly followed by the F.O.B. deciding, after thirty years, to clean out his underwear drawer. Out with the old—many dozens of pairs are ceremoniously dumped in large trash bags—in with the new! Several dozens of new pairs are unwrapped, color coded, laid side by side in the drawer, and *voila*...new beginnings. The next morning at approximately 5:25 A.M., I'm awakened with a tap on the shoulder and invited to view the new full-cut brief. There is a slight problem: the waistband is nestled under the armpits. All several dozen pairs are unwrapped, unfolded, and nonreturnable.

For the remainder of September, if the F.O.B. is seen within twenty-five yards of a mall or a department store, he is to be arrested on sight.

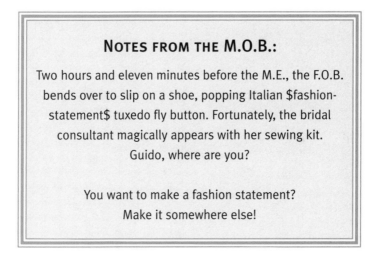

Notes from the M.O.B.:

Two hours and eleven minutes before the M.E., the F.O.B. bends over to slip on a shoe, popping Italian $fashion-statement$ tuxedo fly button. Fortunately, the bridal consultant magically appears with her sewing kit.
Guido, where are you?

You want to make a fashion statement?
Make it somewhere else!

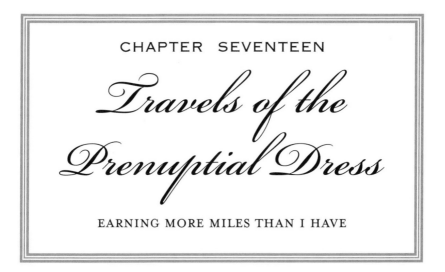

CHAPTER SEVENTEEN

Travels of the Prenuptial Dress

EARNING MORE MILES THAN I HAVE

It is now sixteen days, six hours, and ten minutes before the M.E. I was just told my prenuptial dress left New York one week ago. I must call them back and ask *how* it left New York. Perhaps they put it out on the side of the highway with a sign that said "Oklahoma or bust." Was it on the back of a pony? They said "shipped." Is there a major waterway between New York and Tulsa, or is it bound to go via the Cape of South Africa?

True, I can console myself with the thought that at least this is not the wedding gown, my wedding dress, or the F.O.B.'s clothes. Yet I am becoming involved in the principle of the issue. I want the dress! It has earned more advantage miles than I have.

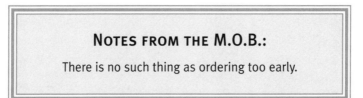

NOTES FROM THE M.O.B.:

There is no such thing as ordering too early.

CHAPTER EIGHTEEN

The Order and Wait Game

IF YOU NEED IT NEXT MONTH, YOU'LL RECEIVE IT TOMORROW. IF YOU NEED IT TOMORROW, YOU'LL RECEIVE IT NEXT YEAR.

I loved the ordering part! It was the waiting I wasn't crazy about. The clothes had their own itinerary. The bridal gown spent twelve days languishing in customs, finally being rescued by Kleinfeld. And then there is the saga of the prenuptial dress—earning advantage miles as we speak.

It is ten days, twelve hours, and three minutes until the M.E.

Hallelujah! The prenuptial dress is in Oklahoma…right color, wrong size. Fortunately too big. Under a death threat, the purveyor has offered to alter it at her expense. Things are looking up. (Hope she doesn't hook up with Guido!)

The only items still touring are several of the groomsmen's tuxedos and possibly some of the groomsmen, having just recently spent the weekend in Las Vegas for the bachelor party. The F.O.B. and F.O.G. are still waiting for their invitations. What a different world today, F.O.B.

laments. "No bachelor party in Las Vegas in my day, just some seedy motel…."

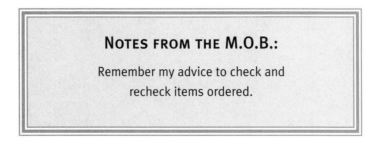

NOTES FROM THE M.O.B.:

Remember my advice to check and recheck items ordered.

CHAPTER NINETEEN

M.O.B.
Underwear

AN EXASPERATING BUT NECESSARY EXPERIENCE

Start early with this category. It's not as easy as you think.

I have spent more time and as much money on alterations of my underwear as I have on the dress.

We have put a man on the moon, but have we invented a functional girdle? No! I have a theory that the same male who designs women's shoes and purses must design her underwear. What does he know from function?

The last real girdle I purchased was when I was in college and weighed ninety-nine pounds and hardly needed one. In eight days, six hours, and seventeen minutes I must look like a pencil; never mind that I won't be able to bend at the waist or exhale. I might try to invent the perfect girdle where form follows function, and function does not require molting of the form.

As for the "merry widow" (where did they get that name anyway?), it, too, has required some major overhauling. I have visions that two hours or so into the reception a ripping noise will shatter the air and bits and pieces of mother-of-the-bride underwear will rain down upon the crowd.

It is seven days (eek!), four hours, and four minutes until the M.E., and I have had one of those rare successful shopping days. I have found a girdle where form follows function; no molting required, although it is a relic from WWII. I have also found a teeny-weeny pair of *pince-nez* (eyeglasses) to go into my teeny-weeny evening bag designed by that previously mentioned male. One must choose between breathing and seeing since *pince-nez* in French means "pinch nose."

I have also found a delicate lace hankie but not a place to put it. A space engineer from NASA will be hired to place each item in my teeny-weeny bag so that it will close. (A source for those teeny-weeny cosmetics to go in the teeny-weeny purse is gift promotions from cosmetic companies, especially during the holidays, such as tiny compacts, mascara, blush, perfumes, etc.) I don't dare open it to fumble around for my hankie when the tears come for fear of never closing it again. As for hankies, the bride has at least four to attach somewhere on her body as she walks down the aisle. They all have sentimental value, having been worn by her grandmothers and the M.O.B. at their respective weddings. She will also have on her person in the pocket of a garter the halfpence my father gave to me when I was married. This clever little pocket hadn't been invented yet on my wedding day, so I taped it in my shoe and limped down the aisle. A second garter for tossing to the bridesmaids will be on her leg so that the one with the halfpence is saved.

I wanted her to carry the Bible I carried at my wedding. She drew the line at that, feeling that she would have to drag a U-Haul behind her.

NOTES FROM THE M.O.B.:

If carrying a purse: after walking down the aisle and
before ascending the pulpit, hand your purse to
someone in the first aisle seat, hopefully to a relative
who will give it back! Your hands will be free to assist
the bride if necessary and to hang on to the F.O.B.

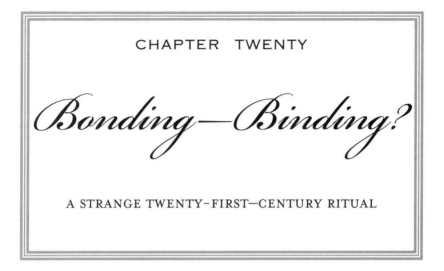

CHAPTER TWENTY

Bonding—Binding?

A STRANGE TWENTY-FIRST—CENTURY RITUAL

It's now fourteen days, eight hours, and thirty-two minutes before the M.E. I have called the B. for the first time today, and I feel I've been put on alert: *Proceed with caution, land mines ahead.* So much for mother-daughter bonding. Now, when talking ten times a day is a necessity, I know I'm going to hear, "We're sorry. You have reached a number that is no longer in service. The new number is nonpublished by owner's request."

Speaking of bonding...the F.O.B. did a splendid thing: he invited the B. to a weekend get-away for a prewedding father-daughter meaningful experience. There is very little room, if any, during the plan-a-thon for fathers and their little girls about-to-become brides to have alone time. (Some might consider this a plus.)

My bride-to-be and my husband went to an island, walked on the beach, reminisced, and allowed me my last sane weekend. I didn't make the bed for three days or answer the phone. I worked on tables at 2:00 A.M. as I bonded with myself.

I can't speak for the B. and F.O.B., but I can say this weekend was a little slice of paradise for me.

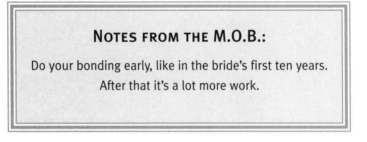

NOTES FROM THE M.O.B.:

Do your bonding early, like in the bride's first ten years. After that it's a lot more work.

CHAPTER TWENTY-ONE

One Week Prior to the M.E.

(Main Event)

THE POINT OF NO RETURN

I am strangely calm. All the important tasks are in the hands of $important$ people. I have reached the point of no return.

It is quiet, save for a strange smooshing, squashing sound…hundreds of thousands of fat cells being flattened, thousands of pounds being shed (mostly in five-pound increments). Hundreds of people slimming down for that pencil-thin dress, that dashing tuxedo.

Personal trainers discover a windfall; tailors find a bonanza. The B. drops another inch, and we have to take the dress down to a size 0.5.

The F.O.B. is frantically searching for a plastic surgeon that will do a combination tummy-tuck and tear-duct removal. The mere mention of the word *wedding* brings on the tears.

My capacity for making lucid decisions is rapidly disintegrating. I know this when the R.O.B. calls to discuss the *Ketubah* (Jewish

marriage contract) signing ceremony, done prior to the marriage ceremony by the bride and groom. The R.O.B. wants to know what color
ink I want for the signing. Black, blue? Do I want felt tip, rollerball,
ballpoint…? I freeze; I become paralyzed; I simply cannot make this
decision. I start mumbling incoherently. "Fine," he says, "I'll bring a
black-ink rollerball pen."

Somehow, deciding on the menus, flowers, and tables was easier than
black or blue ink.

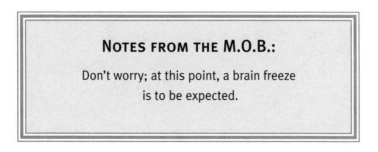

NOTES FROM THE M.O.B.:

Don't worry; at this point, a brain freeze
is to be expected.

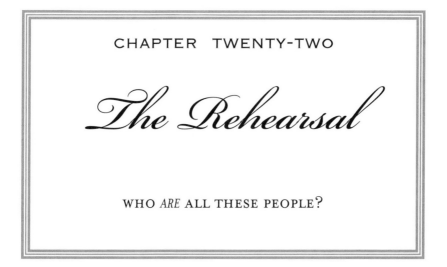

Choreographing twenty-five inattentive postteenagers would test the patience of Mother Teresa.

The boomlet generation (eighteen to twenty-something) is much less neurotic than their parents. Arriving twenty minutes late when there is but one hour to rehearse just isn't a big deal. The best man jogged in just off the streets from a five-mile run. I had to ask the B. who some of these people were—was she positive they were in this wedding?

Between the party planner (me), the rabbi, and occasionally the bride and groom, we managed to create a sensible plan. No one was more surprised than I when the entire ceremony, including processional and recessional, came off without a hitch.

A last-minute addition of two more people made twenty-seven in our bridal party. The groom's step-grandparents attended the photo session prior to the ceremony. Just before we assembled to begin the processional, I was asked if this couple could walk down the aisle with the rest of the family. This would mean six grandparents…a marvelous affirmation of family, when you think about it. "Of course," I said. The florist fortunately had an extra boutonniere, after mistakenly giving my father's away.

This particular couple was the most "chronologically gifted" in their age group. They outlasted everyone at the reception, dancing to the last note. The next afternoon after the M.E., in their spare time, they took in the state fair, rode amusement rides, ate cotton candy and corn dogs, and were ready for another party that night. What night? I cannot even remember that night.

It is crucial to have a processional and recessional script in writing before the rehearsal. Last minute nips and tucks are fine, but flying by the seat of your pants is not! Discuss this beforehand with clergy and the bridal couple. They must know how they want their attendants to walk up and down the aisles, where they stand on the altar, where parents stand, etc.

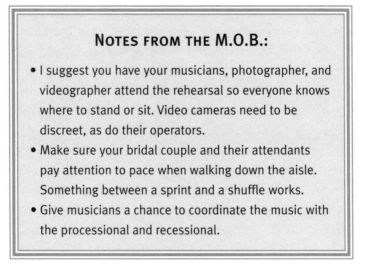

NOTES FROM THE M.O.B.:

- I suggest you have your musicians, photographer, and videographer attend the rehearsal so everyone knows where to stand or sit. Video cameras need to be discreet, as do their operators.
- Make sure your bridal couple and their attendants pay attention to pace when walking down the aisle. Something between a sprint and a shuffle works.
- Give musicians a chance to coordinate the music with the processional and recessional.

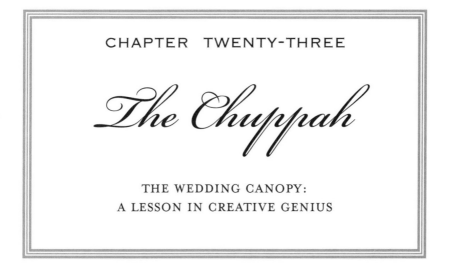

CHAPTER TWENTY-THREE

The Chuppah

THE WEDDING CANOPY:
A LESSON IN CREATIVE GENIUS

The *chuppah* is the canopy under which the bride, groom, best man, maid or matron of honor, parents, and rabbi stand during a Jewish wedding ceremony. Many different designs of this *chuppah* are possible. My B. wanted an ethereal effect, as if she were enveloped in a heavenly cloud. Our florist—an artist of great genius—draped, wrapped, and bedecked this canopy in organza until it took on the magical look of a celestial cocoon. We didn't see it until the rehearsal. I thought he understood that it was just to cover the main players. He thought it was to cover the whole bridal party. I gasped in horror as I realized the error. This *chuppah* looked like a revival tent stretching across the entire front of the room. Knowing his artistic sensitivity, I tried my best to explain to the florist that he would have to shrink this canopy by at least two thirds. All that work—all those magnificent hand-draped organza cabbage roses—had to be redone.

At the appointed hour, our rabbi stood alone under the heavenly *chuppah*, waiting to receive the bride and groom. He is of medium to small stature. Wearing the traditional long white robe—standing with his hands clasped in front—he looked like an angel about to sprout wings and levitate right to heaven through the organza canopy.

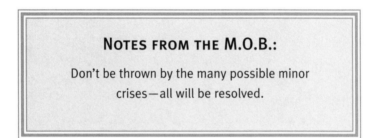

NOTES FROM THE M.O.B.:

Don't be thrown by the many possible minor crises—all will be resolved.

Twenty-Four Hours to Go

THINGS HAVE GONE TOO SMOOTHLY...

We have just returned from the prenuptial party Friday evening. I'm relaxed, basking in the afterglow. We really enjoyed this party that we were not hosting.

Things have gone too smoothly. Something is wrong.

Murphy's Law (if something can go wrong, it will) is lurking nearby, just waiting to ambush me.

Suddenly, my son runs through the house shouting, "Hey, Mom, Dad, can you hear it?"

"Hear what?" we say.

"That dripping sound."

We had suffered rains of monsoon proportions the entire day. Our roof had given up. All over the house, minor rivulets were dripping from the ceiling. Tomorrow is the M.E. Tonight I need my beauty sleep, and I'm racing through the house frantically searching for vessels to catch rainwater. Naturally this disaster is going to require repairs billed at $weekend rates$.

I try to comfort the F.O.B.: "At least it isn't Saturday night when we will be spending the night and next day at the hotel. At least the dogs are boarded. At least your Italian tuxedo didn't get wet."

NOTES FROM THE M.O.B.:

Remember the big picture.

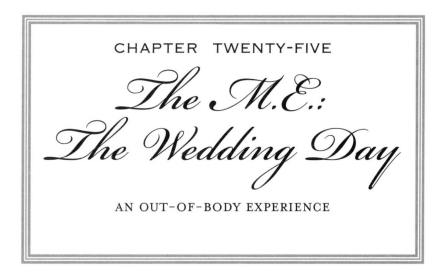

CHAPTER TWENTY-FIVE

The M.E.: The Wedding Day

AN OUT-OF-BODY EXPERIENCE

Somehow, I feel like I'm walking around in someone else's body.

The cast of players comes in and out of our hotel room. I catch brief glimpses of the B. and F.O.B.

The wedding dress is delivered along with the tuxes. Everything finds its way to our room.

The clock is ticking. Soon we are all assembled to be made up, dressed, and coiffed. The mothers and grandmothers are peeking in as the B. is transformed into a fairy-tale goddess. We are lined up, awaiting our turn at transformation.

I help my B. into her gown. The bridal consultant is busy bustling and buttoning, (all those tiny silk-covered buttons up the back of her dress—the groom will have his work cut out for him).

I'm doing my best to remain calm, composed, and in charge.

The B. adjusts her father's bow tie. He becomes misty-eyed. I start weeping. There goes the carefully applied makeup. Someone catches the moment on film.

And then, the moment arrives. The most exciting ride of my life: the ride in the elevator down to the M.E. It takes all four elevators to transport the wedding party. We allow the B. to exit alone; her groom is waiting. This is the first time he sees her bedecked and adorned. They have a few precious moments together. They are moments worth freezing. Fortunately, I arranged for the photographer and videographer—hidden from view of the bridal couple—to capture this treasured scene. I will suggest they watch it on every anniversary.

We have the *Ketubah*-signing ceremony. I'm astonished at how relaxed everyone is. (I discover why later—the mysterious water-like liquid they have been sipping.)

I don't recall my feet touching the ground when I walked down the aisle. I purposely came down first despite tradition so I could turn and watch the entire wedding procession. The moment my daughter entered, a vision in silk and roses floating on the arm of her father, I bit the inside of my cheeks so I wouldn't cry. In fact, I was bursting with joy. The F.O.B. was biting his lip. He and the B. made a pact: if one sniffle escaped, they would both collapse—so no tears!

In the massive wedding party, only one person almost tripped ascending or descending the steps, no one fainted, and the rings and vows were exchanged without a flaw.

While I was under the *chuppah* with the F.O.B., everyone one else in the room seemed to vanish. I felt we were alone in the moment. I heard each jewel of a word from the rabbi.

Once the couple was formally united, exchanged their kiss, and my son-in-law stomped the glass (a Jewish tradition), I stood ready to attend the best party of my life.

Everyone hired delivered his or her best work, from the ice carving–cum–vodka and caviar bar to the band's rendition of my reworded "Oklahoma."

My only wish would be to attend this event again…as a guest.

CHAPTER TWENTY-SIX

The Morning After

"MOM, WHERE'S ALL MY STUFF?"—THE NEW MISSUS

A t 9:30 A.M. the morning after, there is a knock on our hotel door. We open it. Standing there is our breathtaking bride— in a hotel terrycloth robe that is six sizes too big for her, her Contessa coif in a lovely mass around her face, her perfect makeup mussed. In her little, tiny voice she asks, "Mom, did I leave some stuff in your room last night?" The F.O.B. and I heave a sigh of relief; our little girl is not gone after all.

I help her take her "stuff" across the hall to the bridal suite, consisting of several magnificent rooms. The majority of these rooms remain untouched except for a trail of clothes leading to the bedroom. Her shoes in the foyer, followed by her veil, her Kleinfeld creation thoughtfully tossed over a couch, etc.

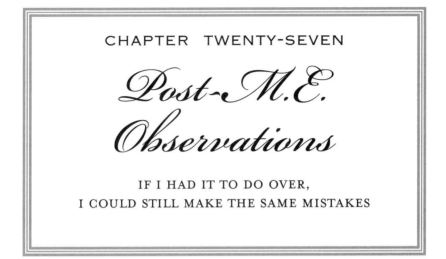

CHAPTER TWENTY-SEVEN

Post-M.E. Observations

IF I HAD IT TO DO OVER,
I COULD STILL MAKE THE SAME MISTAKES

A t the reception, M.O.B. and F.O.B. will probably spend a total of twelve minutes together—part of which will be one dance.

One or both of you will never finish a sentence, let alone a conversation. Said sentence will consist of the same four, five, or ten words, "Oh, thank you so much, we're so glad you could share it…" You will feel like a hummingbird, alighting on a conversation here, there, somewhere else, each for one to three seconds. Your overall impression will consist of mini sound and visual bites.

Your smile will be frozen on your face. The next morning your jaws will ache.

You will rely on the descriptions given by your best friends as to who looked gorgeous, what they wore, how they accessorized. Your very best friends will tell you the truth about the food, flowers, music, etc. "It was so-o-o fabulous, *but*...."

You will be among the N.D.I. (no disposable income), maybe forever....

Remember the tip on no alcohol preceremony? Amazing how innovative young people are today. It seems that a large pitcher appeared in the holding room with the bridal party. It was filled with clear liquid and ice. I saw people taking sips and assumed (dumb me), that it was water. Later I discovered it was vodka—straight. The F.O.B. noticed it and ordered the pitcher out of the room. It reappeared with glasses near a reception table where guests were picking up their programs before going into the ceremony. One of my guests told me how thoughtful she thought it was to have ice-water available...until she took a large swig and blew it out her nose!

As for the seating arrangements, no matter how careful you try to be, how socially clever and correct, you will make at least one faux pas and seat someone next to someone to whom they are no longer speaking.

CHAPTER TWENTY-EIGHT

Post~M.E. Lost and Found Department

YOU DON'T REALLY WANT TO KNOW

- One pair of bridesmaid's shoes
- One black silk slip
- One pair of men's silk pajamas
- One man's watch
- One call from hotel security wanting to know what I wanted to do with these things.

At first I said, "Where did you find these things?" Embarrassed silence. "On second thought," I said, "if anyone really misses anything, they will call you."

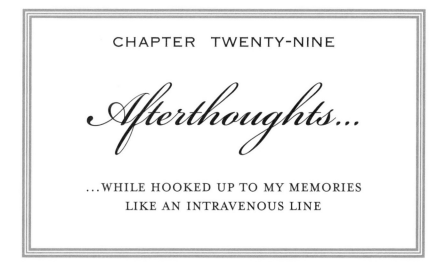

CHAPTER TWENTY-NINE

Afterthoughts...

...WHILE HOOKED UP TO MY MEMORIES LIKE AN INTRAVENOUS LINE

It is eleven days, three hours, and six minutes after the M.E.; I am not depressed, dejected, or downcast. I don't feel let down as everyone said I would. Instead, I am hooked up to the intravenous wedding video, just as I had planned, reliving every $memory$.

The wedding affair was even more fabulous than I remembered, but I only remembered about thirty-five minutes out of eight hours. I did dance once with the F.O.B. I did taste the dinner, even someone else's at another table, to make certain it was delectable. It was superb! I had forgotten the love and care that went into planning the menu. Once we had the tasting, I left that matter behind and moved right along to the next one.

Part of the afterglow is the feeling of satisfaction that your desires were, in fact, fulfilled.

The B. and G. definitely had a party they won't soon forget!

The F.O.B. is now having an acute attack of writer's cramp as all the bills roll in. He's going to hand out take-a-number tickets to the "team" of creditors.

The newlyweds are still honeymooning.

I am paying bills—basics like utilities (somehow we still have water and electricity although these bills were due weeks ago). Remember D.I.N.K.s (double income, no kids) of a few years ago? We are now D.K.N.I.s (double kids, no income).

CHAPTER THIRTY

The Good Stuff

THE THOUGHTS THAT STAY
IN YOUR HEART FOREVER

- The first time your bride is veiled
- The look in her eyes as she sees herself gowned and veiled for *the* walk
- The minutes during the ceremony when it feels as if no one else is there except you, the F.O.B., and the bridal couple
- The bridal portrait, when you can just sit back, watch, and drown unashamed in tears of adoration
- The couple of minutes to dance with the F.O.B. at the wedding; to share your love and joy with the significant other person responsible for your bride. You probably won't cross paths again until it's over
- The few minutes you have alone with the B. before she makes her entrance
- Her walk down the aisle on the F.O.B.'s arm

- The first time the bridal couple is introduced as "Mister and Missus"
- The amazement when it's over that it really worked! All those sleepless nights and days that were too short, worries and wonders (as in "I wonder if...")—and it all came together

CHAPTER THIRTY-ONE

R.U.T.s
(Really Useful Tips)

FINALLY, THE HELPFUL STUFF

REALLY USEFUL TIPS
Your Mantra

Remember, above all, *Whose wedding is this anyway?*

Is a cross word or a difference of opinion so important that you would risk a lifetime of bad feelings? This is the bride's show, not yours. The F.O.B. told me more than once, "If you want to do it your way, have your own wedding!" I am extremely fortunate to have a daughter who understands her mother's quirks and obsessions. Be prepared to listen if you're going to ask for an opinion; otherwise, don't ask. Operate on N.T.K. (need-to-know) basis. Many details do not require a group vote or even a B. and G. vote. You'll have to make some decisions requiring a leap of faith. As Nike says, "Just do it!" and hope the bridal couple won't notice. I made the mistake of asking the groom's opinion of the menu. Little did I know he fancied himself as the next chef extraordinaire! I quickly crafted my N.T.K. policy.

Start a File Early.
I started mine when my B. was twelve days old (just kidding). I collected articles pertaining to all facets of party giving—menus, floral ideas, traditions, music, clothes, etc.

The F.O.B. tells everyone that I have had this wedding planned for fifteen years. Buy a book about your particular religious or ethnic customs and traditions. There is so much to learn.

Buy That Organizer.
Create timelines by working backwards. Eight months ahead (should you be so lucky), start a schedule of what needs to be done each month. The last month prior to the M.E., break the timeline into weekly, then daily, segments. Be sure to check off completed tasks and date them. (See Fig. 5.)

Use Professionals Whenever You Can.
If you do not use a bridal consultant, make sure you have *extra-dark socks, cuff links, panty hose, and sewing kits for the bridal party.* Someone surely will forget something. Be familiar with how to bustle the bridal gown if necessary.

Buy Gifts for People That You Are Depending Upon.
Give them prior to the M.E. Lavish is not necessary; thoughtful is. I found out what my chef's favorite wine was and brought a bottle to the tasting. My catering manager just moved into a new office and needed

some desk accessories. The R.O.B. loves toys, so I bought him an engraved yo-yo. At the prenuptial dinner, the photographer took photos of the hosts and hostesses who entertained for the bridal couple. I put the photos in monogrammed picture frames and gave those as gifts. The following people received either cash tips or gifts:

- Catering manager
- Reservations manager
- Chef
- Rabbi
- Head bellman and valet
- Hair and makeup stylists
- Security

Break In Your Shoes.
Wear wedding shoes and underwear around the house (great photo opportunity) so that you can break them in. You'll be in them for hours at the M.E. This is good advice for everyone in the bridal party.

Have Trial Runs.
If possible, have trial runs with hair and makeup stylists before the wedding portrait. Invite the F.O.B. to the wedding portrait. It will help soften the blow of seeing his precious little girl transformed into a breathtaking, beautiful young woman about to embark on life with another man. He should have special moments with the B. whenever he can. One of my most touching memories was observing the F.O.B., without his knowing, when he first saw his daughter as a bride. We also arranged a few private moments between the B. and G. before taking the wedding photos, which took place prior to the ceremony. Our

videographer captured those precious moments on video, unbeknownst to the about-to-be Mister and Missus.

Compose Your Speeches.
Write toasts and welcoming remarks well in advance and rehearse so you can deliver them calmly.

Organize a Tasting.
Definitely have a tasting with your caterer. Set the table just as it will be for the M.E. This includes linens, folded napkins, china, and crystal. Have your florist bring a centerpiece. It's important to know how much room on the table the settings and decor require. Sample the wines you'll be using. Call a taxi to take you home.

Take Advantage of Local Culture.
If you have out-of town guests, utilize local flavor when you can. Oklahoma is rich in Western culture. I used this theme on stationery for correspondence and schedules, in decorating the hospitality suite, and for other events surrounding the M.E. All of the treats and goodies in the hospitality baskets were made in Oklahoma. Most hotels have magazines that feature articles of local interest. The Chamber of Commerce is a good resource for material such as sites of interest, maps, and history. Most of our out-of-town guests had never set foot in Oklahoma, so we gave them the best Western welcome we could.

Attend to Hotel Arrangements.
Discuss hotel check-in with the reservations manager and the bell captain. You don't want any surprises. I did a person-by-person room

assignment with the reservations manager, eliminating many mistakes in the process.

Use Name Tags.
The night of the prenuptial festivities is usually the first time all the guests meet, so name tags are very helpful. I made tags that were titled F.O.B. (Friend/Family of Bride) and F.O.G. (Friend/Family of Groom). The tags were bordered in blue for the groom's guests and red for the bride's (I couldn't find pink). At a glance, one could see the "connection." Knowing that people don't like pins or sticky stuff on their clothes, I put the tags in plastic envelopes on plastic cords that slipped around the neck. (The rehearsal or prenuptial dinner is a good time to make your "housekeeping" announcements regarding attendants' clothes, rehearsal, schedules, transportation, etc.)

Have Extra Flowers.
Remind your florist to have *extra boutonnières and bouquet flowers* on hand at the wedding in case of emergencies.

Optimize the Photo Session.
Provide a fan at picture taking. It gets hot under the lights. If you're doing photographs before the ceremony, serve light snacks and clear liquids (no alcohol). Salsa and chips are a no-no. Serve finger sandwiches, bottled water, 7 UP, etc.

Assign Tasks.
Make someone responsible for collecting the toasting goblets, guest book, cake knife, bride and groom's cake slice, bridal bouquet, etc. *after*

the M.E., or you may never see these items again. I asked the "head" bridesmaid and groomsman to take care of these duties.

Keep Laughing.
Buy or rent a *Father of the Bride* video. Watch it before, during, and after the plan-a-thon. The bride's in-laws gave it to us the first time they came to town.

Know Your Duties.
To whomever is hosting this gala: *certain honors belong to you*, i.e., introducing the new "Mister and Missus" for the first time, welcoming remarks, the first dance, toasting (try to confine it to the immediate family). Work with the band so that these elements come off smoothly.

NECESSARY CORRESPONDENCE

Write thank-you notes to everyone who does anything for you (baking, assembling, running errands, entertaining, etc.).

Once our out-of-town guests responded that they were attending the wedding, I sent them detailed letters with an event itinerary for the weekend (including attire, although separate invitations were sent for rehearsal dinner, brunch, etc.), hotel arrangements, transportation, and a probable weather forecast. Upon arrival, the hotel placed a welcome "goodies" bag, à la Oklahoma, in each out-of-town guest's room. Included was the weekend schedule, an information packet from the Chamber of Commerce, a guide of special exhibitions and beauty salons, and our phone numbers. (See Fig. 7.)

I enclosed the following information in all the bridal party corre-spondence: rehearsal schedule, where and when to leave bridesmaids' dresses for pressing, where and when to pick up and drop off tuxedos, where and when to meet for pictures and rehearsal. We also arranged for men to have last-minute fittings on tuxedos (very important).

THE INVITATIONS

Buy a pair of cotton gloves at a drugstore. Use them when you handle your wedding invitations and envelopes. You might look silly as you assemble or address them, but at least your guests will not find fingerprints on them. Try to do these tasks in a quiet unhurried atmosphere; this will decrease mistakes.

Remember to take a complete invitation to the post office to determine adequate postage. Oversized invitations require extra postage!

The correct way to assemble the invitations and inserts is as follows:

1. When using a folded invitation, the lettering is on the front, face-up.
2. Place the tissue on top of the text. Place the reception card on top of the invitation, face-up. The response card is placed face-up under the response envelope flap, and the whole thing is placed on top of the rest. Any additional enclosures would be placed on top, face-up.
3. Insert the invitation and all enclosures into the inner envelope, *folded edge first.* If using a flat card, insert it so that it reads right-side-up when removed.
4. Insert the inner envelope into the outer envelope so that the inner flap (loose) faces the front of the outer envelope. When the outer envelope is opened, the names should read right-side-up on the inner envelope.
5. When the entire invitation is assembled, take it to the post office for correct postage. There are very attractive stamps available now. Considerate hosts put postage on the response envelope.

I suggest a fill-in-the-blank response card as follows:

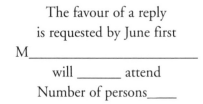

The favour of a reply
is requested by June first
M_____
will _____ attend
Number of persons____

(The "honour of your presence" is requested when the ceremony takes place in a house of worship. The "pleasure of your company" is requested when the ceremony is anywhere else but a house of worship.)

Keep a 3 x 5 alphabetical index file for the "yes" response cards. File the "no" regrets in a different file. Use the cards for gifts received and acknowledged. Or use your data files on your computer and keep your lists there; update them and print them out.

Number the response cards on the back in pencil corresponding to an alphabetized guest list, unless you want to drive yourself crazy trying to figure out who forgot to fill in their names and which postmark they belong to—but are attending. No matter how simple you make it, someone won't do it.

Include "Number of persons ____" on the response card. You'll be surprised how many single invitees will assume it is acceptable to bring a $date$. And for those families with children, if you want the children as guests, put their names on the outer as well as the inner envelope. If you don't believe me, read "Dear Abby" for horror stories involving uninvited guests and little children. I was the flower girl from hell in the wedding of my mother's cousin. I was about four years old at the time. I toddled down the aisle tossing flower petals like a pro. The rabbi bent down to help me, his bushy beard hit me in the face, and I went screaming back down the aisle, almost colliding with the bride. Afterward, that particular relative was never nice to me.

THE TABLES

Seating kits are available through party planners or party stores. They are a huge help in arranging your tables. If you cannot find them, here is an easy way to do your seating:

Buy packages of sticky notes (my favorite invention since sliced bread) in the smallest size in two different colors: one for bride's guests, one for groom's guests. Use regular sheets of 8.5 x 11–inch paper. Write the last names of each guest on the appropriate color sticky note, using one for each unit (a unit being a single person or a couple). Arrange the sticky notes on the sheets of paper in numbers corresponding to your table size, i.e., eights or tens. At a glance you can see your guest "mix." Each sheet is a potential table. Once you are reasonably sure that a table is complete, transfer the names to a seating chart. Write in pencil or have lots of white-out handy (my second favorite invention). Next to the name, you can write in any dietary requests in order to facilitate the servers. (See Fig. 6.)

Obtain the configuration of the reception room with the placement of tables from the caterer; then assign table numbers. Know where the band risers will be and how much room to allow for them, where the cake table will be, and which table will be for the bridal family.

Arrange the guest's names alphabetically with the corresponding table numbers on another list in addition to the seating charts. Make copies for yourself, the caterer, the party planner, the calligrapher (table cards/place cards), and anyone else needing this information. Understand that *at the very last minute* things will change. Be prepared to rearrange those sticky notes. Have extra place cards on hand or with the calligrapher. Once everyone has copies of the seating charts, it is easy to call in changes by table number and/or alphabetical names.

THOSE PESKY BUSINESS DETAILS

Obtain all contracted services in writing—*contracts, signed by all parties, fees and services specified.*

The Band

Exactly how many band members are expected? What equipment will they bring, and what will they need at location? Who is responsible for what equipment? What will they wear? What time is set-up? We had a printed agenda down to the minute: when each course was to be served, when each special event or dance was to be announced, when to take the breaks. Be sure they know how to pronounce the names correctly. I'll never forget a wedding we attended where the new Mister and Missus were introduced by the bandleader. Their names were mispronounced so badly we thought we were at the wrong reception.

The Reception

All food and drink must be itemized. Most prices per person do not include service charges and gratuity. Specify liquor brand names if serving call drinks. Ask that refills on wine at dinner be by guests' request; do not automatically refill glasses.

Be definite about the final head count before you pay the bill. At the M.E., have someone pick up unclaimed seating cards to verify your final count. Under-guarantee by 5 percent. This means if you are expecting three hundred guests, you "guarantee" 285 (i.e., you agree to pay for 285 people minimum). You and the caterer will account for final numbers. Speaking of percentages, expect 15 percent regrets if you have at least 25 percent out-of-town guests, slightly less if all guests are in-town.

The Bridal Consultant

Just what exactly will she do and not do; how many hours will she be needed? This is the person with the emergency sewing kit, extra socks, panty hose, bow ties, bustling expertise, and big shoulders to cry upon. Her duties involve the wedding ceremony and bridal party.

The Party Planner

What exactly will she do and not do; how many hours will she be needed? Her duties begin after the ceremony with the reception.

The Photographer and Videographer

The best way to choose a photographer or videographer is to view sample albums and videos. Ask to see complete weddings from beginning to end. You'll notice "style" when you look at different photographers' works. Make sure the professional has back-up equipment and assistants. Professional photographers usually send their work to binders who fashion the album. Make sure you're familiar with the process.

Insist that photographers and videographers attend the rehearsal. Let them know ahead of time (in writing) of special photo requests. They need to see placement at the ceremony of props and players in advance so that they can position their microphones and other equipment unobtrusively. Check lighting. If the lights are too low, the video will be too dark. If they are too bright, it will look like a theater during intermission.

Take along a camera for candid shots during planning—the wedding-dress search, fittings, florist, etc. Your bride will have a wonderful keepsake of all the preliminary stages of planning.

Place disposable cameras (they come decorated for weddings) at tables during the rehearsal dinner and wedding reception, allowing guests to take candid photos. Some folks think the cameras are favors to take home, so it's a good idea to be specific with instructions.

The Florist

Present a budget, and *stick to it.* This is one area where it is so easy to go wild. My B. wanted cascades of white roses in October (of course). I had forgotten in all the excitement that I was highly allergic to roses. I was reminded by my runny nose and elegant sneezing during dinner. My florist created the illusion of roses aplenty without having each and every flower a white rose. His eye was so critical to me that I asked him to attend the tasting as well as the rehearsal.

Don't forget the emergency extra boutonnières, corsages, and bouquet flowers.

Checklist for Your Photographer/Videographer

These people may be your most important choices. Their work will provide you with archival memories of this most extraordinary day. If the photos or video are failures, you will regret it. There are no retakes!

1. Check references. Carefully view their finished product.
2. Understand the contract and the different photo packages.

3. Who will be the photographer at your wedding? If possible, get it in writing. You don't want substitutes.
4. Check out sepia and black-and-white photos. They have an air of timelessness about them and have become quite popular again.
5. Insist that the photographer and videographer attend the rehearsal. They need to know where to stand, put equipment, etc.

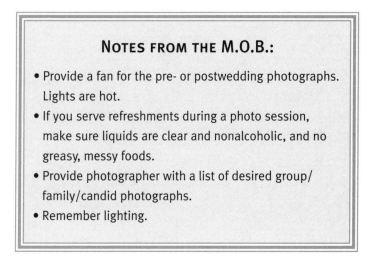

NOTES FROM THE M.O.B.:

- Provide a fan for the pre- or postwedding photographs. Lights are hot.
- If you serve refreshments during a photo session, make sure liquids are clear and nonalcoholic, and no greasy, messy foods.
- Provide photographer with a list of desired group/family/candid photographs.
- Remember lighting.

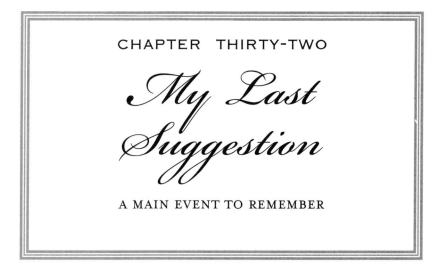

CHAPTER THIRTY-TWO

My Last Suggestion

A MAIN EVENT TO REMEMBER

Have fun. Have faith. Be kind to yourself. Take up yoga; it's wonderful for mind and body. Hold on to your sense of humor and your family (especially the B. and F.O.B.). Promise yourself your M.E. will be a day and night to remember!

Wedding Budget Breakdown

RECEPTION 50%
Site, food, bar, cake, rentals (determined by time of day, number of guests, type of menu, liquor or not, formal seated dinner versus informal buffet, etc.)

BRIDAL ATTIRE 10%
Gown, headpiece and veil, shoes, jewelry

Music 10%
Ceremony and reception

Photography 5–10%
Photographer, videographer, albums, portraits

Flowers 10–15%
Ceremony (bouquets, altar décor, aisles), reception (table centerpieces, cake table, etc.)—category most likely to be carried away! Proceed with caution!

Miscellaneous 10%
Bridal stationery (invitations, thank-you notes, table cards, wedding programs, monogrammed napkins), calligraphy, postage, favors and attendants' gifts, transportation, consultant fees

Average breakdown at one hundred dollars per guest, seated dinner. Buffet with less alcohol, morning or noon reception, would break down at less per guest.

Bride's Budget Planner

ITEM	BUDGET	ACTUAL COST
Wedding Dress:	$	$
Headpiece and veil		
Shoes		
Lingerie		
Jewelry		
Accessories		
Florist:		
Ceremony		
Reception		
Photographer:		
Videographer:		

Invitations and stationery:		
Wedding programs		
Thank-you notes		
Personal correspondence		
Wedding ring for groom:		
Lodging for out-of-town bridesmaids (if necessary):		
Attendants' gifts:		
Trousseau:		
Reception:		
Site rental		
Caterer		
Food and alcohol		
Wedding cake		
Groom's cake		
Table linens, napkins, and monogrammed paper napkins and guest towels		
Decor other than flowers		
Music/Entertainment:		
Ceremony		
Reception		
Officiant's fee (often split with groom):		
Miscellaneous:		
TOTAL	$	$

Groom's Budget Planner

ITEM	BUDGET	ACTUAL COST
Jewelry:	$	$
Engagement ring		
Wedding ring		
Wedding attire rental:		
Ties or accessories for men in wedding party		
Florist:		
Bride's bouquet		
Ceremony flowers for aisles, pews, altar		
Boutonnieres for men in wedding party		
Mothers' corsages		

Gifts:		
Bride		
Groomsmen, ushers		
Lodging for out-of-town groomsmen (if necessary):		
Clothes for honeymoon:		
Marriage license:		
Bachelor party (often given by groomsmen):		
Prenuptial dinner (usually given by groom's parents):		
Honeymoon:		
Officiant's fee:		
Limousines:		
Miscellaneous:		
TOTAL	$	$

FIGURE FOUR

Floral Budget

Description	Number	Cost each	Total
Bouquets:		$	$
Bride			
Bridesmaids, headpieces			
Flower girl			
Toss bouquet			
Corsages:			
Mothers			
Grandmothers			
Boutonnieres:			
Groom			
Groomsmen			

Ushers	
Fathers	
Ringbearer	
Grandfathers	
Décor:	
Altar and aisles	
Ring bearer's pillow	
Flower girl's basket	
Cake table	
Guest-book table	
Seating-card table	
Reception Room:	
Table centerpieces	
Head table	
Stage	
Miscellaneous:	
TOTAL	**$**

Sample Monthly "To Do" List

THINGS TO DO FOR THE MONTH OF AUGUST

ITEM	FOLLOW-UP DATE
Discuss ceremony details with rabbi	8/2
Make B. hair stylist and makeup appt.	
Mail invitations:	
*out of town (6–8 weeks)	8/15
*in town (5–6 weeks)	8/22
Order napkins, guest towels, programs	
Meet with florist	
Call buses for transportation	
Meet with hotel	

Sample Seating Chart

Event _____

Date _____

Table # _____ Number at table _____

Table Name _____

Special Dietary Requests:

1. Mr. Alan Bergane _____ Vegetarian _____
2. Mrs. Susannah Koffe _____ Kosher _____
3. _____ _____
4. _____ _____
5. _____ _____
6. _____ _____
7. _____ _____

8. _____   _____

9. _____   _____

10. _____   _____

Sample Letter to Out-of-Town Guests

Dear Friends and Family,

We are delighted you will be joining us in [city] to celebrate [bride] and [groom's] wedding.

The weekend plans will include:

Friday evening, 7:30: Prenuptial dinner hosted by [groom's parents] at [place address]. Dressy attire, invitation to follow.

Saturday morning, 10:30: Services at [church or temple] with lunch following hosted by [hosts]. Transportation will be provided.

Saturday evening, 8:00: The Main Event! [place] Black tie.

Sunday morning, 10:00: Brunch at [place] hosted by [hosts]. Travel-casual attire. Invitation to follow.

The hospitality room will be in the [Regent's Suite (floor)], opening Friday afternoon. Come by for a snack or a chat.

We have set aside rooms for you at the [hotel] (reservation cards enclosed). Please make your reservations by [date]. Tell the reservations department you are with the [bride's last name–groom's last name] wedding party.

October in Oklahoma is usually the best time of year; crisp, sunny, and cool. We can't promise, but we can hope!

The hotel has airport shuttle service, available by calling from the baggage-claim area.

We look forward to sharing this exciting weekend with you.

[Bride's parents, Bride and Groom, Groom's parents]

Sample Schedule of Events

5:15 Bride arrives at hotel (Church, Temple, Mountain, etc.).
      Party planner or bridal consultant arrives at hotel.
      Bridesmaids, house party arrives at hotel.
      Groomsmen, ushers arrive at hotel.
      Photographer and videographer arrive at hotel.

5:30 Photos begin in ballroom.

7:15 Photo session ends.

7:30 Seating music begins.
      Ushers in place to escort guests (hand out programs, etc.).

8:00 Ceremony begins.
      Put sign on easel outside door saying no one will be seated
            until bridal party has completed processional.

8:30 Ceremony ends.
      Cocktails and hors d'oeuvres served.

9:00   Salad preset before doors open to dinner in ballroom.

9:15   Band starts playing.

Doors to ballroom open and waiters ring chimes for guests to be seated.

9:20   Parents, bride, and groom go to anteroom.

Bar in cocktail area closes.

9:25   Bandleader introduces parents of the bride.

9:35   F.O.B. introduces bride and groom as "Mister and Missus." Newly marrieds join parents.

F.O.B. makes welcoming remarks, introduces rabbi.

Bars in ballroom open.

9:40   Everyone is seated for first course, salad presentation.

10:00   Entrée is served (wedding party tables served last).

Bride and groom dance the first dance.

Parents join in.

Wedding party joins in (band takes fifteen-minute break after this song).

10:35   Dessert is served.

10:45   Everyone is served glass of champagne.

Toasts begin, F.O.B. first.

10:55   Bride and groom called to bandstand for their remarks.

11:15   Bandleader announces cake cutting (band takes fifteen-minute break).

11:30   Band resumes playing.

11:45   Bandleader announces garter and bouquet toss.

About the Author

Sherri Goodall knows from whence she speaks. She owned a party store for several years in Tulsa and was a sought-after party planner. The ultimate test came when she planned her daughter's wedding in 1994. Utilizing her creativity to the maximum, she unearthed the most efficient and effective ideas and resources necessary to produce a wedding unique to the bridal couple…a wedding with panache, dazzle, sophistication, and originality.

Goodall was among the wedding-planning veterans on weddingdetails.com. Her expert M.O.B. advice was sought by hundreds of inquiring brides, their moms, their grooms, and others concerned with the M.E. (the Main Event).

Goodall is the Editorial Advisor and a Contributing Editor for *Oklahoma Bride Magazine*, which debuted in January 1999.

In August of 1998, Goodall became a M.O.G. (Mother of the

Groom) and found that she could wear beige, but keeping her mouth shut was a stretch. (There is a well-known maxim among wedding literati that mothers of the groom are expected to wear beige and keep their mouths shut.)

Goodall is a freelance writer, specializing in travel. Her articles have appeared in several publications including *Departures*, *Travel News*, *Nostalgia*, and *Tycoon* magazines. She writes for *Tulsa People*, *Tulsa Kids*, and *Tulsa Woman*. A grandmother of three, Goodall has written several humorous essays on grandmotherhood, which have appeared in *50 Plus*, *Metrofamily*, *55 and Better!*, and *Senior Magazine*, to name a few.

"I have ridden elephants in Chiang Mai, tuk tuks in Bangkok, hot-air balloons over Kenya, camels in Eilat, rafts on the Colorado River, the Eastern Oriental Express through Malaysia, cabs in reverse in Mexico City (when the transmission ran in one direction only—reverse)," says Goodall, "but the most thrilling ride of all was the one in the elevator down to my daughter's wedding!"

Goodall graduated with a Master in Fine Arts and has had careers as a graphic artist, art therapist, art-gallery owner, real-estate agent, willing  traveler, and participant in community activities. Sherri loves to explore new fields of endeavor and has recently taken up tap dancing and boxing—neither of which threaten her "day job."

She is married and lives in Tulsa with her husband, two Westies, and a ceaseless imagination.

Her newest book, *Wedding Details FAQ's: 101 Answers to Your Top Wedding-Planning Questions*, was released in March 2002.